NAGAUTA
The Lyrics of Kabuki

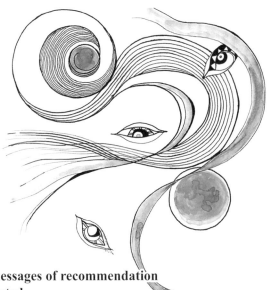

Nagauta lyrics, messages of recommendation and profile translated
by Ariyoshi Okumura

Other translation
by Akiko Yamaguchi

Edited
by Jenny White

Illustrated
by Mika Katayama

MIYOSHI
Art Publishing

NAGAUTA
The Lyrics of Kabuki
Contents

Kabuki and Nagauta
                            by **Ariyoshi Okumura** *3*

For the Extraordinary Goal Okumura-san Challenges!
                            by **Yoshiharu Fukuhara** *4*

Depuis si longtemps ……
                            by **Toru Haga** *6*

Nagauta finally becomes readable as an easy language
    Congratulations on the completion of its Translation into Modern Japanese and English
                            by **To-on Toru Ajimi** *10*

Emitting the Fragrance of Japanese Culture into the World
                            by **Rikutaro Fukuda** *12*

Like a lied by Franz Schubert
                            by **William P. Malm** *14*

    Supervisor : Profile of **To-on Takeshi Minagawa** *15*
    Supervisor : Profile of **Louis-François Duchêne** *16*

                    Preface by **Ariyoshi Okumura** *17*

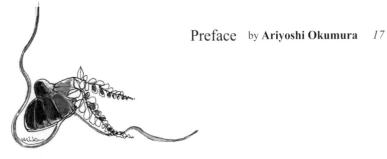

38
Urashima
—*A New Ode to the Sea*
(Shin-kyoku Urashima)
新曲浦島

43
Thrust and Parry Sequence
(Ikioi)
いきほひ―菊寿の草摺り―

48
**The Mad Woman
  of the River Sumida**
(Shizuhata-Obi)
賤機帯―隅田川辺の狂える女人―

55
Chikubushima
—*Bamboo Island in Lake Biwa*
(Chikubushima)
竹生島

60
Horai Mountain
—*A Holy Palace*
(Horai)
蓬莱

64
The Egret Lady
(Sagi Musume)
鷺娘

69
Combing Black Hair
(Kurokami)
黒髪

73
A Love Mound in Toba
(Toba no Koizuka)
鳥羽の恋塚

84
House of Tsuna Watanabe
(Watanabe-no-Tsuna no Yakata)
渡辺綱の館

90
**The Ghoul
  of the Adachi Plain**
(Adachiga-hara no Kijo)
安達ヶ原の鬼女

101
Frog
(Kawazu)
蛙

106
A Puppeteer
(Kairaishi)
傀儡師

111
Lion Dance in Echigo
(Echigo no Shishi-Mai)
越後の獅子舞い

117
The Opulence of Kinokuni-ya
(Kibun Daijin)
紀文大尽
―紀伊国屋文左衛門の豪遊―

126
Utsubozaru
—*The Monkey and the Quiver*
(Utsubozaru)
靱猿

135
Evergreen Pine
(Matsu no Midori)
松の緑

139
The Tale of the Seawater Drawers of Suma Beach
(Shiokumi)
汐汲み

145
Willow Trees on the Bank
(Kishi no Yanagi)
岸の柳

149
Benkei on Board
(Funa Benkei)
船弁慶

161
Lions—*Father and Son*
(Ren Jishi)
連獅子

166
Dojo Temple of Kishu
(Kishu Dojo Ji)
紀州道成寺

174
Girls in Blossom Season
—*Wasting Time on Their Way Home*
(Tenarai-Ko)
手習い子

180
A Circuitous Path to Revenge
—*The Story of Kuranosuke Oishi*
(Uki Daijin)
有喜大尽―大石内蔵助物語―

192
Dirty Spider
(Tsuchi Gumo)
土蜘

201
Devil Fox in China
(Sangoku Youko Monogatari)
三国妖狐物語

208
The Fisherman and Woodcutter
(Gyoshou Mondou)
漁樵問答

214
A Scouring Rush Picker
(Tokusa Gari)
木賊刈り

218
Autumn Grasses
(Aki no Irokusa)
秋の色種

223
The Wisteria Woman
(Fuji Musume)
藤娘

228
The New Year Lion Dance
—*Section 1 : A Girl Page*
(Kagami Jishi)
鏡獅子 （上）小姓の巻

Acknowledgments
by **Ariyoshi Okumura** *236*

Ariyoshi Okumura
——*Profile*
238

Copyright © 2015 by Ariyoshi Okumura

Illustrated by Mika Katayama, © 2015

Printed in Japan
MIYOSHI KIKAKU (MIYOSHI Art Publishing Co.,)
A-102, 1-162, Shin-matsudo, Matsudo
Chiba-ken, 270-0034 JAPAN

TEL.(81-47)347-3211 FAX.(81-47)347-3222
http://miyoshikikaku.com

ISBN 978-4-938740-99-3

Kabuki and Nagauta

by **Ariyoshi Okumura**

Kabuki is a uniquely Japanese theatre, developed during the Tokugawa period (1603?-1868), originally by a legendary woman dancer Okuni and then popularized mostly by male players. It catered to the interests of the new merchant class arising in this lengthy period of peace, and to the stoic, aesthetic and ethical values of the citizens in the towns. Even today Kabuki theatre is very popular in Japan.

Naga (long) uta (song) was the lyrical poetry that complemented to the main accompaniment music in the later part of the period. Precise data and the complete works of Nagauta music in English was available in a new book published, written by Dr. William P. Malm, Professor Emeritus, School of Music, Michigan University, USA.

For the Extraordinary Goal
Okumura-san Challenges!

by **Yoshiharu Fukuhara**
Honorary Chairman, Shiseido .Inc.

Why, Okumura-san sounds as if he is a cultured man, older than me, though actually both of us belong to the same generation!

He studied at the College of Arts and Sciences at the University of Tokyo. So it is no wonder that he deserves his high reputation. Having said that, he is undoubtedly outstanding.

In addition, he commands a high skill of the English language, drilled into him when he served in the unforgiving and harsh world of financial business in Wall Street. When he came back home, he swiftly changed his life style, being awakened by Japanese traditional art, particularly by the beauty of Kabuki dancing and of its lyrics, mostly written in the form of Nagauta.

According to his recollection, his mother had strongly urged him to start its practice as soon as possible, or life is too short to reap its joys. His English translation of Nagauta in this book naturally reveals his enormous concentration and dedication in this direction.

Coincidentally, I myself also started to practice Nagauta when I was six years old. It was June the 6th. This mysterious 6-6-6 number was the long-established habit of when to start traditional lessons, particularly for small children of wealthy families in downtown Tokyo. I still keep the memories of some lovely phrases, without then knowing the mature meanings of the lyrics. I flattered myself then, that I could be a fine master of singing some day! But the War era had broken my dream.

Okumura-san describes how he hopes that the translation might help to convey the traditional feeling of Japanese Kabuki lyrics to those children once taken abroad with their parents and that have come back home without any exposure to their indigenous culture. However he even seeks to go further to deepen his understanding of Nagauta through the process of translation.

Okumura-san is an active contributor of a magazine, named *Hohozue* published by a group of business people. I am sure that his outstanding ability could create an original Nagauta lyric from his own aesthetic idea. Then I would be more than happy to sing it with my recovered "virtuoso" voice!

Depuis si longtemps ……

by **Toru Haga**
Professor Emeritus, the University of Tokyo

Ariyoshi Okumura, translator of this book, was a very precocious boy as far as I recall. He had an outstanding knowledge about all categories of music and seemed to be aware of the sensual joy coming from musical sonority. Also he was keen about linguistic finesse. Therefore it was always enjoyable to listen to his talk in his sweet and slightly foggy voice.

More than half a century ago, we were a little over twenty years old, and fresh-faced students at the newly established Department of Humanities and Social Sciences at the College of Art and Science at the University of Tokyo. I chose the French culture course and he did the English one. Some of our colleagues covering both courses decided to publish a coterie magazine which was in fact made of a very poor quality paper reflecting the time of postwar hardship. But engaged in the editing work together of this magazine, our friendship became still closer.

Since we lived nearby, we visited each other frequently. At his home, he pleased me by playing Fauré and other composers

Depuis si longtemps ......

on the cello. At my home, we were charmed by 78rpm classical records including the music of Mozart and Chopin, though they even included folk songs such as "Donna Mariquita!" Even today when I am relaxing in a hot bath, I still hum those tunes.

It was indeed since we spent quite a lot of time listening to many records together in my small study that I came to realize and admire this round-faced young boy, Ariyoshi Okumura, and how he captured the essence of western culture and of music in particular.

Recently, I opened with nostalgia the said coterie magazine *Kaju* (Flower Tree) in which such names as Shuji Takashina, Sukehiro Hirakawa and Susumu Kawanishi are found. All are graduates of the same middle school attached to the Tokyo Teachers Education Institute. It was to my renewed surprise to notice that in the first volume, published in February 1952, Okumura-san contributed an English translation of a short stanza from *Makura-no-Soshi* (The Pillow Book) written by Sei Shōnagon.
It goes as follows:

"The moon shines serene.
As my carriage is wading the brook slowly

Led by the cow walking gently
Stream splashes at her foot
　and bears crystal fragments.
It's amusing!"

In fact he recreated the stanza into elegant English poetry even with some spontaneous refrains in it. I felt he was a really precocious and exquisitely sophisticated guy, intoxicating and fascinating to us all.

In the days of 1950's some Japanese were too much influenced by Western culture. Okumura-san on the contrary, was able to tackle such an illustrious and authentic essayist as Sei Shōnagon in a smooth and insouciant manner.

More than half a century has passed. Okumura-san now publishes a unique translation of Nagauta into English. His achievement seems to me to be simply the return to his own genesis.

'Urashima' (A New Ode to the Sea), 'Kurokami' (Combing Black Hair), 'Shizuhata-Obi' (The Mad Woman of the River Sumida), 'Sagi Musume' (The Egret Lady) etc., all illustrate this achievement.

Depuis si longtemps ......

After finishing his activities in the globalized financial world, Okumura-san returned to his original nest with the aim of conveying the traditional essence of Japanese humanity to a global audience. As a Japanese, to have taken this step and dedicate himself to such an inspiring new lifestyle, is surely a cause for celebration.

Nagauta finally becomes readable as an easy language
Congratulations on the completion of its Translation into Modern Japanese and English

by **To-on Toru Ajimi**
President of Nagauta To-on Society,
Professor Emeritus, Tokyo University of the Arts

Looking back over my long career as Nagauta Shamisen player from when I was five years old, I am really surprised of the length of the time that has passed.

The learning of English was not generally introduced in school education until the end of World War II. As it rapidly became fashionable, I dreamed, as a student of Tokyo University of the Arts, of the day when Nagauta would be finally translated into English so it could be widely appreciated among a global audience who are interested in Japanese traditional entertainment, such as Kabuki as well as Nagauta.

In fact, however, any translation is so difficult to achieve and so my naive thought at that time withered and vanished.

A half century has passed since then. Okumura-san has challenged this impossible dream and started to introduce a series of those translations in a coterie magazine, *Hohozue* containing the English translation of thirty major pieces with excellent notes and the modern Japanese language as well. It removed all the trouble of reading esoteric texts in the old Japanese language.

Actually Okumura-san also sings Nagauta rather well and more importantly digests the meaning of those lyrics deeply.

I would suggest firstly, Japanese people are welcome to read and enjoy its lovely translation, and then invite foreign friends who love Japanese entertainment to join you.

Someday Okumura-san and his mentor, To-on Mr. Takeshi Minagawa would sing Nagauta with my Shamisen accompaniment.

My dream is ever expanding.

Emitting the Fragrance of Japanese Culture into the World

by **Rikutaro Fukuda (1916-2006)**
Professor Emeritus, Tokyo University of Education

The 2004 Nobel Prize in Literature was given to Ms. Elfriede Jelinek, an Austrian Novelist. It reminded me of the case of the Japanese Prize Winner, Yasunari Kawabata in 1968.

At the request of Society for Promoting Japanese Culture, I wrote an essay then, on the overseas response about his winning the prize, to the effect that how I was deeply moved by reading the editorial of a Dutch paper the *Algemeen Handelsblad.*

They insisted that in selecting a Japanese writer, the policy of the Nobel committee was not an effort of discovering an unknown renowned individual, but of recognizing first of all, Japan as an nation with a great cultural tradition in literature, and the fact that no Japanese writers had been awarded in the past was totally unacceptable, equally so if no French or British authors had won the prize.

These words were surely heartwarming.

We should not forget, however, Japanese writers are destined to be handicapped with its language, a most impenetrable one, unknown in the world. So the essence of the traditional fragrance of Japanese culture, including Kabuki and Nagauta, is tightly sealed in such a difficult language. In this sense, the venture of Okumura-san in translating Nagauta into English is really a most gallant enterprise.

Okumura-san is a successful businessman in an international arena. He is a good example of having his own colorful talent as well as outwardly emitting the cultural vitality of Japanese people.

As he expresses in his own writing, Nagauta is indeed a pretty flower in the unique garden of Japanese culture. His excellent translation reveals its beauty, and hopefully will shed its blossom to a global audience.

As a student of the same reputable Japanese literature, born in the same country, I would thank him for his marvelous effort and hope he will further deepen the understanding of traditional culture in this country and the world as well.

Like a lied by Franz Schubert

by **William P. Malm**
Professor Emeritus, School of Music,University of Michigan, USA

Franz Schubert wrote many famous songs (lied).
When you buy copies of them, their words usually appear in at least two versions, the original German and then English, French, or even Japanese.

Through the diligent work of Ariyoshi Okumura, Nagauta texts also are now equally available to the international repertory of famous songs. His book contains lyrical English language translations of important compositions plus historical details, drawings, and the original Japanese text.

Both Japanese area scholars and general musicians must thank Mr. Okumura for this important addition to our appreciation of an important genre of Japanese dance and concert music.

Like a lied by Franz Schubert

Supervisor

Profile of **To-on Takeshi Minagawa**

Born in 1935 in Nihon-bashi, Tokyo. He practiced Nagauta as an in-house apprentice of Yuzo Nishigaki, who was Professor Emeritus of Tokyo University of the Arts, later a Living National Treasure. He became an independent soloist singer in 1980 and joined To-on Kai, a leading group of professional Nagauta singers. He is now a managing director.

In 1988 the Japan Culture Promoting Association awarded him for his contribution in international activities.

His singing well succeeds an orthodox savour of the late professor Nishigaki and attracts many lovers.

Supervisor

Profile of **Louis-François Duchêne**

Born in 1927 in London. He studied at the London School of Economics.

After coming back from military service, he became a correspondent of the Manchester Guardian and then an economist at the European Union. He was an ardent assistant of the late Jean Monet for some time.

While he spent an academic life at the Royal Institute of International Affairs and also at Sussex University, he played an active role in the cultural exchange group between Europe and Japan and was indeed interested in Japanese traditional culture.

His works include *Jean Monet*, 1994 and *Essay on W. H. Auden*.

He passed away in 2005 at the age of 78.

Preface

by **Ariyoshi Okumura**

(1)

Japanese classical art performances developed, matured, and then probably over-matured together with Kabuki performances since earliest times. Our classical art performances have bloomed like a flower preciously nurtured inside the hothouse of Japanese culture. It blossomed in the soil of Japanese language and aesthetics, in the garden of our "complete insider system" with the background of Japan's national isolation during the Edo era.

When a modern Japanese person takes a step out of this 'insider system' to travel, live or study abroad, or try to build business relationships with foreigners, or even fall in love with or be married to a foreigner, he gets a chance to think of his identity and realizes that he has been living in an unique cultural garden. This shocks him, and makes him feel ashamed of having been ignorant of Japanese culture. The renewed curiosity about his own culture is then vigorously awakened.

Such a new appetite for learning about his own culture does not allow him to fall into mere self-satisfaction, but transforms into a new impulse to convey such knowledge to his beloved family, friends, and all those who are interested in Japan.

This is the motivation that drove me to translate Nagauta songs, firstly into modern Japanese (Japanese translation is not read in this edition) and then into English. There are many people whom I wish to read this book. The first group is the Japanese brought up abroad and have returned to Japan. Another group is those who are enthusiastic to introduce Japanese culture to people outside Japan, and also those who wish to know more about Japanese culture including Japanese living abroad and foreigners who are interested in Japan.

I brought up my three children, who are now adults, outside Japan. I am very much concerned with how to enlighten those who were brought up outside Japan with the essence of precious Japanese classical art performances and the atmosphere they evoke, which they had missed the experience of when they were young.

In the 1960s, Japanese industry and educational institutions started to send out a large number of business people and scholars with families abroad, and naturally the number of 'returnees' to Japan drastically increased. Half a century after the boom, some of those returnees have now returned abroad, and others have opted to stay in Japan. However, it is this generation who are now the new leaders of our society, both economically and culturally. I would like to present this book of Nagauta songs translated into English to those returnees.

You may say "Nagauta? What is that?" That is quite understandable. Nagauta songs were quite popular among the generation of your grandparents, or maybe your parents if they were interested in Kabuki. However, with the increase of nuclear households with no elder generations living under the same roof, culture is no longer passed down through the generations. Now that the broadcasting of classical art programs on TV or radio has become a rare occurrence during peak-time viewing in the evenings when most people watch or listen, and hobbies have diversified, classical art performances are marginalized to the edge of mass media. I also suspect those who were brought up with protein/fat rich food of western culture abroad may not find it easy to accept this 'low cholesterol type' Japanese classical art.

Yet one's tastes change as we grow older, whether these are for food or art. When you start to feel fed up with the taste of butter, please have a good look around you. There are still quite a lot of people who enjoy traditional classical Japanese art performances, including those who also enjoy English culture at the same time. I know a good friend of mine who runs a company sending out simultaneous interpreters and loves Nagauta. If you visit Nagauta performances presented by professionals, you will find large venues quite full of people enjoying the evocative melodies of Nagauta.

To my regret, when young, Japanese people tend to split into two groups: those enthusiastic in pursuing only Western culture, or the other, albeit small in number, only interested in Japanese culture. These two groups of Japanese are completely separated like oil and water, and form completely different social cultures. I find this is a great misfortune for the future of Japanese culture.

I believe returnees with their linguistic skills are in the best position to bridge the two divided social cultures in Japan, as they can approach Japanese classics with the fresh eyes of foreigners. The same can be said for the increasing number of foreigners with fluent Japanese and a good basic knowledge on Japanese culture. I hope Japanese classics once loved by our ancestors will be appreciated with fresh enthusiasm.

However, foreigners and returnees who had spent their youth overseas, especially in developed countries and enlightened by Western ideas, might have a negative reaction against the male-dominated current of Japanese classics in the feudalistic Edo era. In my opinion, however, such prejudice found in our classical art performances is not a perpetual one, although it was quite a common theme during that particular transitional historic stage of civilization. Therefore, I wish readers of this book not to be too caught up with the gender aspects. Rather, I encourage them to transcend such superficiality to reach the core of the Nagauta songs introduced here and find the cries of the human soul in pursuit of unique aesthetics in the songs while struggling under restrictions imposed by their social frameworks.

Some foreign students studying Japanese classic literature in Japan have even started to translate Kabuki and Nagauta. I consider it my duty to endeavor to keep up with the efforts of such people by reintroducing our own culture, and hope my small contribution through the book will serve as a part of this synergy. Mr. James Brandon who was a cultural attaché working for the US Embassy in Tokyo devoted himself to help develop Japanese classical art researchers and art lovers as a Professor of Drama of the University of Hawaii. I feel grateful for his zeal and feel that we have to do our fair share in doing the same.

Nagauta is a popular genre of music that flourished alongside

Kabuki plays from the mid-18th century. Shamisen is a three string Japanese guitar that accompanies Nagauta songs, and is noted for its transparent and clean-cut tunes. Shamisen music by ten or so musicians lined up on a spectacular stage creates such a special grand atmosphere and I am sure there are a lot of people who have had a mesmerizing experience listening to the Shamisen music played on the Kabuki stage called 'Kanjin-cho.' The same is said not only for listeners but also for Nagauta singers themselves. Nagauta singers singing out loud from the bottom of their bellies on stage wear family crest-bearing kimonos (called Montsuki) and pleated skirts for men (Hakama). This is their on-stage uniform and they do not wear top coats (Haori, a kind of formal jacket to be worn on top) for some reason or other. Strangely enough, they are also not required to make any bows before or after performances, which is surprising considering it is such a habit in Japan. Do they not have to bow because Nagauta is the pinnacle of all Japanese classical musical performance? Does the fact that they do not have to wear Haori jackets on the stage imply that they are trying to be casual despite the fact that they are the top performers of classical music? We are not sure of the philosophy underlying such habits.

This book is dedicated to the pursuit of literalistic essence rather than to any academic study of Nagauta. Before going on to the main part of my introduction, I would like to apologize to those who are interested in the study of Nagauta, for whom the book may not be satisfactory.

(2)

My Childhood Memories

It was one day during a rainy season in June. I was eleven years old and had just moved from a primary school in Kobe to one in Tokyo. I could not speak the Tokyo dialect and could not keep up with my sharp witted classmates born and raised in Tokyo, and so I was in a kind of depressed mood. As I walked in the rain with an umbrella, I saw a grand house encircled by stone walls of perhaps 1.5 meters high. A large garden inside was well preserved and raised from the ground level and I could only glimpse a part of it. There were no other passers-by, and I was surrounded by the quiet sound of rain. Through the wet air, there came a delicate sound of Shamisen, as if it reached me like a thin string through the atmosphere.

After many years, I came to know that the house belonged to a famous Nagauta instructor. The scene is still vivid to my senses: a large garden protected by thick aged trees, drizzling rain and wet air, Nagauta Shamisen music reaching me as if coming out of rain drops falling from leaves ... Old cherry trees lining the street in the front of the house then are now cut down, taken over by fresh young trees. The house itself is also

23

gone, and probably due to our heavy inheritance tax, the land has now been split up into small areas where small houses are built. My first and precious memory of Nagauta is thus lost forever.

Sendai-hira (a kind of Hakama) and Hairy Shins

The biggest expense I had to make when I started practicing Nagauta was for the purchase of Montsuki and Hakama. First, I called a kimono tailor who had long been serving my family to order Montsuki made of finely woven glossy black silk. My family crest is rather a flamboyant one symbolizing a peony flower called 'Tsugaru-Botan.' I have heard that our traditional family crest used to be different, but there is no longer a way to check that, because all my older generations are gone. What I do know is that my father's mother did not like a simple crest for the family and changed it to the present one which she thought looked better.

Once when I mentioned that our crest was 'Tsugaru-Botan' to a politician from Tsugaru district (presently Aomori Prefecture), he was so pleased and shook my hand many times vigorously with his big and rough hand, probably because he thought we were from the same area. We may have our origin in Tsugaru in some way, as our ancestor is said to be a warrior called Shigenari Kimura, who served the house of Toyotomi, defeated by Ieyasu Tokugawa, who later became of first Shogun of Edo era. It is said that when the house of Toyotomi lost its rule over Japan, our ancestor escaped to Ō-shu (north of Japan, Iwate Prefecture), where our family name Okumura derives from. If this is true, then our family may have some relation to Tsugaru district as the two districts are nearby each other. In any case, the 'Tsugaru-Botan' crest has now become our true family crest, as it has now been within our family for more than 100 years.

The next thing the tailor asked me was what sort of Juban (an under-kimono) I wanted. When he noticed I was mumbling not knowing what to say, he said, "I recommend GIN-NEZU (silver mouse) color." I could not understand the meaning of this word, although it made me think of the color of a silver fox (GIN-GITSUNE). In the end, I decided to leave everything to the professional, which turned out to be the right idea. The set of kimono he suggested looked very nice on the stage. Japanese people traditionally are sensitive to color. It sounds much nicer to express 'gray' as 'silver mouse.' I imagine professionals all over the world are distinguishing subtly different shades of the same color by giving different names, as I have encountered names like 'moss green,' 'olive green,' or 'avocado green' in the U.S.

The next problem was the choice of Hakama. The tailor told me to choose 'Sendai-hira.' An expensive looking wooden box he brought over to me had something written on it in black ink. "Isn't this expensive?" I asked him gingerly. He looked at me solemnly and said, "Yes, the person who wove this is going to become a living national treasure, so certainly another zero would be added to the end of the price." This was the most persuasive comment and I almost gave up resisting him, but had to ask again. "What makes expensive Hakama different from the cheap ones?" His answer was very clear. "Cheap Hakamas fold tight when you sit down. Therefore, when you stand up after sitting for a while, the hem does not fall down immediately and reveals hairy shins. You see, like an accordion." Since hearing that laughing comment, every time a performance is finished and singers stand up, I look around to check if I see if there are any shins revealed, hoping this would not be happening to any of co-singers around me.

(3)

My First Performance and the Late Mr. Yuzo Nishigaki, my grand Mentor

The year after I started to practice Nagauta singing taught by Mr. Takeshi Minagawa of To-on, I had my first experience of singing on the stage. It was a casual performance wearing Yukata (casual summer cotton kimonos) held in August 1976 and the song was 'Echigo-Jishi' (Lion dance in Echigo). It was the time when I was practicing hard in a mist without knowing where I was going and what to do. I was often teased then that my Karaoke sounded like Nagauta, and my Nagauta sounded like Karaoke.

When I was on the stage for the first time, Mr Yuzo Nishigaki, who was then a Professor Emeritus of Tokyo University of the Arts, sang with me. I still feel very sorry that I had had no idea how great a singer he was then. However, his character and dignity was very impressive. I was very tense to be sitting on a high performing stage laid with red carpet, called *Yamadai*. The podium felt so high, as if I were standing on a diving board. I felt shaky and scared if I would fall down from there on my head. When the curtain started to rise, Mr Nishigaki whispered to me: "Let's enjoy singing." His words relaxed me and I was sincerely grateful that I had such a nice teacher.

The song 'Echigo-Jishi,' the first Nagauta I sang on the stage, became something like my first love. I nostalgically think back of my childhood days, when my great uncle, a Nagauta lover, was singing this song when he had a bit too much to drink.

(4)

Nagauta and Popularization of Noh

Generally, even today, Noh seems to be considered the most sonorous performance because of its profoundness and subtlety, followed by Kyogen which has more comical elements than Noh. Nagauta however, has always been ranked behind the two as popular art loved by commoners. As this ranking is based on a long-lasting belief of ours, there would be no point in raising any objection to this. The fact is, probably Noh and Kyogen were ranked higher than Nagauta in the past, as they were sponsored and protected by the Shogun and Daimyo (local lords serving Shogun), whereas Nagauta was loved and nurtured by commoners and 'littérateurs.' In old times, for the snobbish elite of politicians ruling the country, Nagauta may have been an artform to be enjoyed as a secret pursuit.

Yet, Nagauta has certainly established itself as an art to be enjoyed and has gained social recognition. I suppose this is mainly because historically, it developed closely attached to the dances in Kabuki.

In a purely personal view, there are three basic genres in Kabuki plays:1) somber plays with historical soldiers as heroes (such as legends of Yoshitsune, a tragic hero killed by his elder brother who became a founder of Kamakura Shogunate in 12C), 2) gorgeous and rather wanton plays centered on female figures often involving their male partners, originating from the first Kabuki dancing by Okuni of Izumo (a legendary female dancer), and 3) plays featuring monstrous apparitions and dark spirits opposing authorities represented by Samurai soldiers.

I think the three elements above, of 'soldier,' 'female' and 'apparition' were brought to maturity through Noh plays and then became the main elements of Nagauta. I imagine it is not unnatural to think that Noh players who lost their patrons at the end of Edo era looked for a new direction as Nagauta players.

How do we interpret the fact that Department of Nagauta (now called Department of Japanese Music) was set up in Tokyo University of the Arts (then called Tokyo Music School) while there was no Department of Noh and Kyogen? I guess that it was because the intellects of the day considered Nagauta as the most authentic and central Japanese music.

**'Jo, Ha, Kyu' (introduction, explosion, and rapid finale:
An artistic modulation in Japanese art performances)
And 'Otoshi' (coda)**

Nagauta songs do not last long. The longest ones would last for half an hour, while short ones only last for six to seven minutes. However, each Nagauta song contains a whole story and drama. Mountains, rivers, habited countryside or woods, appear in the songs, and an apparition disguised as a small girl comes out after dark. A song may start very slowly and quietly, but at the point where an audience is feeling relaxed, unexpected turnings could then follow. After a stormy climax, a happy ending may await. Sometimes, after a quiet and peaceful introductory part, a song roars like vigorous Niagara waterfall, and then finishes by presenting before the audience again, a scene reminiscent of the calm surface of deep water, as though all movements are completely forgotten.

In general, Nagauta songs tend to end with a perception of the evanescence of life, which, I feel, is a unique sense of beauty commonly shared by Japanese classical art performances including Noh and Nagauta.

This perception of the evanescence of life is like a huge lull. It sometimes appears from the cracks of one's emotional disturbances, and also could put an appearance among the conflict of human relationships or in adversarial relationships between groups. The lull is a universally existent quiet force that overwhelms and devours all states of flux.

The perception of the evanescence of life, however, is in no way a sense of a void, nor is the generating abyss likened to a huge empyreal doodlebug which sucks in everything like a black hole. If we liken the black hole as a 'black emptiness,' the Japanese perception of the evanescence of life may be a 'white emptiness.' Without the power of the 'white emptiness,' or the 'quiet power of lull,' nothing in this world will fluctuate or move on smoothly, whether it is a human sentiment, human relationships, corporate organization, or society. Those who practice Nagauta sincerely with zeal will always be impressed by the sense of the evanescence expressed in the last part of the songs, which may be the greatest virtue of practicing Nagauta.

(5)

The Charm of Nagauta Music

As it is not easy to get hold of Kabuki tickets these days, the lucky person who could manage to purchase them will try to open his eyes as wide as possible to see as much of the magnificent stage plays as he can. However, there are some who prefer to close their eyes to concentrate on listening to the music played on the stage. Although those may be small in numbers, it is amazing to know that such Nagauta fans do actually exist.

There are two elements to enjoy in Nagauta music. One is the grand effect of the orchestration on stage. The beautiful and magnificent musical effect of 'Kanjin-cho' or 'Kagami-Jishi' is beyond description. *Shamisen* performances are not divided into parts as seen in western orchestras and are mostly performed in unison, yet the sound of ten *Shamisen* instruments played together is quite powerful. Percussion instruments like Tsuzumi (a hand drum) mingle into the main *Shamisen* melody haphazardly using double or quadruple beat, and singing is added on top of that. A subtle harmony between such music by the instruments and singing is unique to Nagauta and cannot be attained without year-long experiences on both sides. I sincerely agree with the novelist Kafu Nagai, who praised highly the orchestration effect of Nagauta performance in 'Kanjin-cho' in his essay.

The second element to be enjoyed is the unique construction of Nagauta, with its song and *Shamisen* music as one. While performed using completely different tunes and rhythms, they create an original polyphony when they are together. This is completely different from the polyphony of western music where phases are shared between the two, as Japanese musical effects contain a lot of artifice. If you are a Nagauta teacher, you are required to play the entirely different melodies and beats at the same time: those of *Shamisen* played by hand and of songs you sing.

The same applies to students. As they listen to their teacher, they would have to distinguish the singing part and *Shamisen* part, learn the different tunes and rhythms separately and then combine them again in their mind. I always admire the complexity of Nagauta and think it is the fruit of human curiosity and an inquiring spirit. The more complex the process of learning is, greater is the joy of conquering difficulties, and one would find it impossible not to go further and further. This would probably be the same for work and play.

The Style of Performance is the Reflection of Character

The late Mr. Hiroaki Kikuoka, Professor Emeritus of Tokyo University of the Arts, was a true master of the *Shamisen* for Nagauta as well as a man of great character. Once when we were having dinner together, he told me that the style and taste of performance are ultimately the reflection of one's character. I have always kept his words in the bottom of my heart.

The word ART ('geijutsu') in Japanese is indeed comprised of two characters in Kanji meaning 'flavour of performance' (gei) and 'technique'(jutsu). There is no art if either of the two is missing, but the matter becomes more difficult and at the same time more interesting when yet another element of personality is added to that.

The mention of the importance of personality by someone like Mr. Kikuoka who had mastered the technique of *Shamisen* almost to perfection signifies a lot, whereas the same words coming from someone with no technique would have sounded awkward. What I can do to follow his words is just to repeat in my mind "character, character" as if chanting sutras to remind myself of the importance of cultivating my personality as much as possible. This is something even a lay person like me can do to improve my art of Nagauta.

A professional Nagauta performer would have to put priority on the improvement of technique as he would be doing it as a profession. However, we lay people, are practicing Nagauta for our own pleasure's sake, and do not have to teach its technique to anyone. Therefore, I think we do not have to struggle to master the technique. Rather, once the general technique is acquired (or once we start to realize how difficult it is to perform Nagauta and what a fearful task it is to tackle), we had better try to create our own style. Yet, for us, this again does not mean how to appeal to our audience; we do this just for the sake of self-evaluation and to recognize it by ourselves.

The process of learning Nagauta for us would be: 1) to acquaint ourselves with the entire song (the knowledge), 2) to actually sing the song (the practice) and 3) to reach a kind of completion, satisfactory to oneself (the realization of self). It may sound a bit arrogant for a non-professional like me to talk about 'completion,' but the word 'completion' here includes a 'completion called incompletion.' That is, when we know the limit of our ability, we become humble enough to get the true sense of what I call 'completion called incompletion.'

Although we are far from completion, we, lay people practicing Nagauta, should repeatedly and sincerely ask ourselves the question of whether we are being able to express some of our individuality or unique essence as human beings in our performances, even just a little.

In Japanese society, it is considered polite to pay compliments such as "It was a splendid performance" and the ones being praised to reply humbly saying "No, no, it was not good at all." Although such traditional politeness may be something to be treasured, we also have to ask ourselves quietly whether we could have had expressed the essence of our own as much as our still-to-be-improved techniques allowed. If we neglect doing this, there will be no progress in our mental maturity.

Those who would silently reply to such inner questions of ours are teachers, and also the images of precursors including the deceased. Human beings can only achieve self-improvement when we are in the circle of other human beings. I feel keenly that our progress only becomes possible when we are surrounded by the image of our precursors who have excelled in the art of Nagauta.

NAGAUTA
The Lyrics of Kabuki

Urashima—*A New Ode to the Sea*
(Shin-kyoku Urashima)
新曲浦島
Lyrics by Shoyo Tsubouchi
Music by Kangoro Kineya V and
Rokuzaemon Kineya XIII

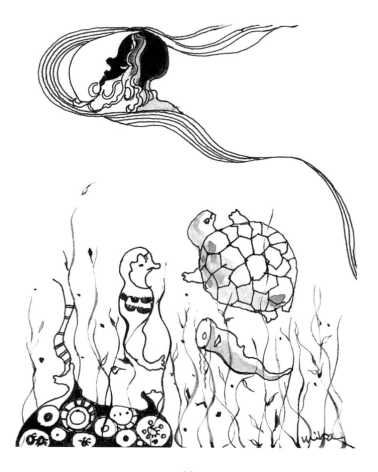

Urashima—*A New Ode to the Sea*

Most of these lyrics are dedicated to the descriptions of the sea. This ode, in fact, is a prologue to the grand drama of a famous Japanese legend regarding the fisherman Urashima Taro.

After describing many facets of the sea... its vastness, depth, beauty and rage... the Urashima fable, in which a fisherman meets a giant turtle and is invited to a dream world under the sea, is unveiled. The magical story of the Urashima fable is foreshadowed by the description of the profundity of the ocean.

The lyricist, Shoyo Tsubouchi, is a well-known intellectual of the Meiji era. Deeply versed in both Japanese and Western culture, he is particularly famous for the achievement of translating the complete works of William Shakespeare into Japanese. He was not only a master of English literature, but a great lover of Japanese traditional performing arts with roots set deep in Japanese literature. Thus, his translation of Shakespeare's works is complemented by his deep background in Japanese culture and tradition.

This Ode was chosen as the first in the collection as it seemed suitable for introducing the world of Nagauta to the new generation of Japanese, returnees from abroad in particular. Good luck everyone!

Urashima—*A New Ode to the Sea*

Waves of the sea come close and draw away.
They hold the divine note of the First Day
Aloof from the dust of the world.

Yes, east of the Bokkai Sea, light years away,
Stretches an abyss no man can see
The Generating Void that sucks in all the waters
From the eight corners and nine
  segments of the heavens.
Like the Silver Lane of Stars the waters stream and stream
  into its depth an endless flow,

And still this great sea, brimming and unchanged,
Defies all limits and abounds.
Chinese sages divined it long ago that vast horizon
  of the Void to which my insight almost reaches.
Looking north, another ocean fills the view merging
  with the far end of the sky.
And in-shore waves, a smoky blue
A blue dispersion into fog
Swallow the shadows of white sails;
Three and five appear and fade away.

Urashima—*A New Ode to the Sea*

Are those really sails, are our eyes deceiving us,
  or are they gulls off shore?
Look, they splash out of the sea.

Misty splashes rising off white horses
Coming close in and wheeling far out
Sheer to that island of Three Peaks
Where an immortal dwells above the curse of aging?

Turn to the west coast and its setting sun
Amidst the mournful air of autumn.
Waves groan, run close into the rocks
Explode and then give up as if serene;

And look out into the far end of the sea where waves
Hive off at morning far as the Korean shore and
Linger there in the evening too.

The setting sun is a regal giant who draws the darkness
  out of night
Across the gold threads of the sky
The footlight coloring and weaving the last curtain
  of the day.
Who is fishing there?
The moon shines pale, remote as a crystal bowl.

And the twilight rim of the sky creeps stage by stage
  from purple to a strip of crimson.
Look! A first star shimmers, can you see?

Laces of cloud scatter and surely
Capricious change is in the air for this autumn sky.
Winds blow: clouds fly with growing agitation;
Fishing boats head home.

  (Sailing Song)
Rain! Go rain and rain,
But wind! No more raging, please,
My man is a sailor and could be your victim.

If the wind speaks, though, let her convey
My words to him.
Wind, can you then blow around him,
My courier, could you do that for me, please?

Sailors' chanteys echo uneasily through the cries
  of the wild geese
When storms begin to blow against the harsh rocks
  of the bay in unrelenting fury.
Lord, oh hear me please.

Thrust and Parry Sequence
(Ikioi)

いきほひ―菊寿の草摺り―

Lyrics by an anonymous writer
Music by Shojiro Kineya I

In the old Edo era, the story of Soga (in which the Soga brothers avenge their father by slaying the foe that murdered him) was loved and considered auspicious as the first drama of spring. Its themes of righteous revenge provided catharsis to the masses burdened with the struggles of everyday life under the strict feudal system, and was enjoyed, as it continues to be to this day, as a tradition accompanying the New Year celebrations. Every good catharsis needs a buildup to give it some palpable tension, however, and one brilliant example of this was the 1788 rendition of 'Ikioi.'

Also known as 'Kikuju no Kusazuri,' or 'the magical armor-padding,' it depicts the impulsive Soga brother, Goro-Tokimune, in a hot tempered determination to avenge his father as soon as he comes across the opportunity. A beautiful woman, who happened to be sitting nearby and knew the rash Tokimune, tried to stop him because the occasion was premature. As a result, a struggle ensues between the fierce samurai and the fragile beauty, in which the woman acquires the magical powers of the undergarments she is wearing, which happen to be the armor pads of her master, the famous general Asahina.

With the hope that Tokimune would consider avenging his father on a later date, she stops him in the name of good timing and noble stature in his execution of revenge. The New Year crowds who were entertained with fantastic costumes, the unexpected wrestling of the sexes, and their annual dose of righteous revenge, must have drunk all the more from the excitement of this play. It is thought to be one of the most popular hits of the late 18th century, and a fine example of what might be called the Spring Fever variety of Kabuki.

Thrust and Parry Sequence

Soga-no-Goroh, or Tokimune
A renowned young warrior in town,
Wearing armour fit for a hero
Resplendent with butterfly designs,
Met a villain warlord in a gathering
Quite by chance and was about to rush
Upon him to avenge his father.

"Not now, do not die," cried a beauty,
Known to all as Shoshoh of Kewaizaka,
Dressed herself in a sumptuous costume
Patterned with cranes
That proclaimed the fame of General Asahina,
From which she drew his power
In clinging to Tokimune's sleeve.

What a breach of natural law it seems
To be halted by a fragile beauty not a steely Samurai!

Rope twined from the black hair
Of women has elephantine strength.
Possessed of that elemental power she tried to hold him
And still was pushed aside,

So great was the fire of vengeance
Stored up in his long-nursed desire.

"This is no drawing-room charade, so leave me!"
"Never, no!"

When morning comes with snow,
There's no way but to stay with me.
It would be totally uncouth to leave
With this early morning rain.
Remain with me a little while.
Was the written oath not to change
Your pledge to me a lie?
Can any lie and a true heart
Exist together in oneself?
Snowed up with pretty creatures
In other gardens do you cheat me then?

Look at you; such a screwed-up face
Spitting harsh words in fury.

Even if you are not plain with me,
I shall be plain with you;
You are my only prop and stay
For the ever-lasting future.

Thrust and Parry Sequence

The insurmountable energy vested in General Asahina
Was transfused through her dress to a frail Shoshoh;
The dance of their thrust and parry moved everyone
Irrespective of nobility and standing.

The Mad Woman of the River Sumida
(Shizuhata-Obi)
賤機帯―隅田川辺の狂える女人―
Lyrics originated from a Noh song
Music by Saburosuke Kineya IV

The Mad Woman of the River Sumida

This is a story about a woman who has gone insane after her child has been kidnapped. Originating from the Noh play "The River Sumida," it was composed as Nagauta in 1829.

A mad woman looking for her kidnapped child wanders about the banks of the Sumida River during cherry blossom season. A passing boatman decides to amuse himself by saying that he would tell her where the child has gone if she is able to collect all of the blossoms floating down the river.

Believing him, she lunges at the water in a desperate attempt to collect the passing petals. Regretting his poor sense of humor, the boatman tries consoling her but to no avail. Not able to hear him, she wanders off after the petals, held fast by the dance of insanity.

The Noh song, 'The River Sumida,' is said to be based on the legend of 'Umewaka Temple' from the Muromachi era (1336-1573). A young boy, Umewaka-maru, lost his father and was sent to a temple, but ran away because of unbearable bullying from other boys, and was eventually kidnapped. Arriving at the Sumida River, he fell ill, was abandoned by the kidnapper and died. People living in the area took pity on him and buried him by the riverbank, planting a willow tree there and building the 'Umewaka Temple' in his memory.

However, the story of this Nagauta is quite different from that of the 'Umewaka Temple' legend. It is also unknown why the song is titled 'Shizuhata-Obi,' originally meaning a sash made of woven hemp (Shizu). Most likely, the poor-quality sash is intended to symbolize the tragedy of the insane woman who lost her child.

In either case, the thrust of this song is contained in the striking contrast between the pitiful sight of a disheveled mad woman scooping flower petals from the water, and the glorious beauty of the surrounding scene: the steaming Sumida River in spring, lined with cherry trees in full bloom. It is concluded with the theme of compassion, as passers-by compare the lost boy with the Umewaka of legend, and join hands in prayer. It is a masterpiece bound to strike a chord in the heart of all those who have children.

The Mad Woman of the River Sumida

The River Sumida, famous in the Azuma
Winds across the plain of waking spring
From Musashino to Shimousa.
Still capped with snow, Mount Fuji
Rises framed in cherry blossom.
To the north Mount Tsukuba sinks afar
Barely concealed by willow sprouts.
Purple mist, eddying in layers trail up to an old ferry
Wrapped round in spring's brocade.
Here must be that site where flocking gulls
Stirred our poets long ago.

Under the peaceful mist of spring
A woman who has lost her mind
Wanders in the fret of her despair
Unsettled as the white water of cascades,
Her nerves so raw she would cover her ears
At the whisperings of bamboo grass.

The sweet flower she could conceive
Her child, was taken from her, kidnapped
Never to be seen by her again.
How can she believe in a God of mercy now?

The Mad Woman of the River Sumida

Her helpless wanderings have no end.

Shall I seek aid from the boatman of a ferry floating by the
  River?
How and where can I begin to find
My fairest one so brutally abducted?
By now her mind is almost blotted out,
Buried in the cloud of madness.
Vacancy creeps behind.

The uncomprehending boatman
Stared and held her in derision;
"Look at this woman! She's quite mad!"
Scoffed at her with nasty claps.

The woman in her turn stared back at him;
"What? Am I mad? What a thing to say!
How can you claim I alone am mad?
Aren't cherry blossoms mad to bloom
At the peal of temple bells?
Waves mad to be whipped up by the gale?
Butterflies made mad by yellow petals?

I wish this beautiful embroidery of three enchanting patterns
Could have dressed my child

51

Put on with my untold caresses.

I am so uneasy and impatient

Haunting this River so far from my goal.

Or may the River be a crevice to settle my child's fate?

What grief if it were."

Her search strides on in vain.

"Where can I find the child? Please tell me, please."

The unfeeling boatman teased her again:

"Hey, look! Use your net and scoop

As many petals as you can,

Then I will tell you where your loved one can be found."

"Really, scoop so many petals? Then let me do it at once

And scoop up petals for my child."

A chilly wind, without knowing

Why the craving in my bosom

Collects so many floating petals,

Sprays me with foam from the white horses.

A touch of sympathy, I beg of you!

The black hair of the mad woman blows about,

As sea-gulls leaning off the shore suddenly fly and scatter.

No one shows the slightest care.

But now the boatman suddenly has a flash of insight and
　　stands up.
"Whom on earth are you looking for?
Whose child? Your child……?
You really do look miserable
Wandering round and round in search."
But this fellow-feeling found no echo.
"Let's dance! Let's dance!" she cheered,
Beating an imaginary drum.
"Brace up your spirit and let's dance!"
And she marched off, deep into the fog.

The beauty of the spring
Springs thoughts too full for utterance.
Mountain cherry flowers through the mist,
Yoshino cherry flowers massed like clouds,
Weeping cherry flowers rumpled
By the wind, like rapids of the swift Yoshino,
Young cherry flowers, the tenderest,
Double-petalled cherries, emblems of tumescent love,
The feast of single-petalled cherries;
With these the grace of spring ascends its peak.

The sense of chagrin and compassion

That has deified Umewaka-maru,
The kidnapped and deserted boy,
Fragrantly spreads far and wide
Reaches out to the remotest villages
Dispensing mercy and benevolence.

Today is a festival at Hie Shrine,
Where a crowd longing for divine favour,
Jostle, enjoy Shinto music, and
Pray for lasting peace in this rough world.

Chikubushima—*Bamboo Island in Lake Biwa*
(Chikubushima)
竹生島
Lyrics based on a Noh song
Music by Rokuzaemon Kineya XI

'Chikubushima' is a remote island surrounded by steep cliffs floating in the beautiful Lake Biwa. Upon it stands a shrine dedicated to 'Ben-Zai-Ten,' the goddess of poetry and the Japanese equivalent to the Greek Muse.

One spring day, a travelling pilgrim hired a fisherman's boat to visit the island. Approaching the island, he saw a young woman amidst the pine trees - a strange sight since women were forbidden on the sacred grounds. The fisherman explained that the woman was indeed none other than the Goddess Ben-Zai-Ten herself. The deeply moved pilgrim watched as the woman disappeared into the shrine only to reappear in her divine form, as a luminous dancing goddess with flowing robes, manifesting music and flower petals from the surrounding moon lit skies. Once the dance was over, a magnificent dragon appeared from the lake where the fisherman had been. The fisherman was in fact an incarnation of Ben-Zai-Ten's guardian spirit, the dragon. Displaying gold, silver and jewels, the dragon offered them to Ben-Zai-Ten and pledged his vow to protect the faithful. The pilgrim was struck with a deep gratitude and devotion towards the great Goddess.

The poem originates from a Noh song which was rewritten in 1862 as background music to a Kabuki dance performance.

Chikubushima—*Bamboo Island in Lake Biwa*

Lively as a nightingale bred in the bamboo forest,
I set out for the shrine on the Bamboo Island.

The scene of blessing is fresh as always in this devout
  excursion;
The site in the lake is in easy reach.
All aboard the pilgrim boat!

Amid the ripened spring in March
Mists of early morning trail across the lake.
As I brood on the wake of brother boats
  overlapping all around,
A touch of awe wells up and haunts me.

My captain, an old fisherman,
Long settled in the hamlet by the shore
A life consumed in catching fish in countless baskets,
Guides me on the sacred way.

A chilly gale blows down
From the height of Hiei mountains
But we are nothing daunted; our barks multiply instead.
Journeys entice anyone; noble and commoner alike,

They sit, packed cordially together,
Making friends spontaneously on board.

Look! The Bamboo Island glides ever closer.
"Here we are, pilgrims. Step ashore."

What a mysterious site this is;
How can a woman possess this island from which her kind
Are supposedly debarred?

"So says the common rumor
Displaying little knowledge of the cult;
For she is Benzai Ten, the Kushou Buddha Reincarnate,
One of his female avatars.
Even as pine trees without any human emotion
Can commune with one another
Despite being planted back to back.
Ben-Zai-Ten appears as an angel maiden
To show the mercy of knots for couples in love,
The aegis of providence."

All of a sudden, the sacred presence seen
In the shade of pine trees
Vanished behind a door of the shrine
And the fisherman also disappeared
As if swallowed up in the depth of the lake.

Chikubushima—Bamboo Island in Lake Biwa

Stricken with pious awe
The pilgrims behold the epiphany
Of a dazzling Buddha by the trees.

The shrine begins to rumble Ben-Zai-Ten appears,
As the sun and the moon rise at the edge of the mountain,
And says:

"Know that I am Ben-Zai-Ten who dwells in this island
To worship the Gods and to protect mortals."

Supernal music strikes up and echoes round the space;
Blossoms float through the twilit air;
Sleeves of the angel gleam in the moonlight
As if 'at the still point of the turning world.'

Then as time returns the festal music fades away.
The dark surface of the water suddenly shudders
And out of it surges the Dragon God who lives at the bottom
of the Lake

And humbly presents to the shining Ben-Zai-Ten gold and
silver and jade.

What a miracle of virtue such an incarnation is!

Horai Mountain—*A Holy Palace*
(Horai)
蓬莱
Lyrics by an anonymous writer
Music by Rokusaburo Kineya IV

Horai Mountain—*A Holy Palace*

Mt. Horai is one of the three holy mythical mountains of Chinese legend. In this poem, Mt. Horai is likened to a 'Kuruwa,' a traditional Edo era red-light district where men were entertained by a sophisticated ambience of otherworldly art and beauty. Such a metaphor may seem strange to a modern day audience, but is very common in Japanese traditional performing arts.

An additional legend explains how once upon a time this song was performed for the blessing celebration of a newly built noble-man's house. However, the home burned to the ground very shortly after the celebration. The family members suspected that a curse was placed on the house by the verse "Salt ovens are yet smoking," and hence came to detest this song. We may enjoy it even more, however, if we consider the Buddhist teaching inherent in this legend as well as in the song itself: that impermanence stands ready to reduce a world of beauty to ashes, that all forms are indeed empty of inherent existence, and that all worldly pursuits are ultimately futile.

Horai Mountain— *A Holy Palace*

Filtered sunshine lingers between leaves
And lights up the blossoms on each blade,
Beckoning us as a sheaf of sirens
Wearing a harvest of golden clothes.
Feathery breeze, you are a seducer!
My Obi might blow away.

The sun is setting but as salt ovens are yet smoking
Along the sandy beach,
My bosom keeps flaring for love instead.
Who could tame such an emotion?
My pillow never be quiet night by night,
As a rock tossed under angry waves.
The vain talk of affairs takes wing abruptly
As birds, home sick for the nest,
Make lustfully for the mountain of love.

Pretty bush clovers bending low with silvery dews
Barely waken to the early morning quiet
As my sleeves get wet with farewell tears
In the bed of entwining meory
Full of clinging flesh and perfumes.
Who could escape from such bonds?

Silver grasses waving in the wind
Raise their arms seducing me.
Yellow flowers, purple flowers,
You are all together luring me
Into the garden of intoxication.
How could I ever leave this trance?
Only as murmurs vapor into air.

The hilltop contours of this holy palace

Recede into the mist of height and distance,

The saintly refuge of the legends

The Horai mountain the serene abode.

Pine trees, shapely branches, emanate a grace aloft

Embracing noble cranes

Whose fingers dancing amidst the needles,

Seem to pluck a harp.

The Egret Lady
(Sagi Musume)
鷺娘
Lyrics by an anonymous writer
Music by Yoshiji Fujita

The Egret Lady

This song was written in 1763 to accompany a Kabuki dance routine. Several versions exist, and numerous Kabuki masters have added variations on the dance, which gradually developed into a classic and sublime form.

A white egret standing by the waterside on a snowy winter day is used as a metaphor to describe a beautiful young girl agonizing over illicit love. From the title, one might think that it was something like a Japanese version of Tchaikovsky's 'Swan Lake,' but it turns out to be a very different storyline.

It is a ruthless story of a girl who suffers from forbidden love and goes to hell as a result. Her life was not without bliss and color, however. She experienced the joy of falling in love, the difficult emotions of trying to win a man's heart (as difficult, says the song, as making sea-salt by pouring bucket after bucket of seawater onto beach sand), and the hot embarrassment of losing oneself in passion and throwing herself into a man's arms despite the watchful eyes of passersby and the gossip stories that would surely result. Like the memory of going cherry blossom viewing on Mt. Yoshino and catching blossoms blown by the wind in her kimono sleeves, her life was full of transient pleasures and colorful emotions. But only the suffering of hell awaits her in the end.

One may ask whether this kind of eschatological view is commonly portrayed in classical Japanese performing arts. The message of this play could be seen as a teaching to enjoy the moment while it lasts, making the best of one's life situation despite its transience. Or it could be a harsh warning that one should live life with the reality of a catastrophic end stoically in mind.

Whichever the case is, we must admire the authors' imagination and creativity through which the simple sight of a white egret led to a dramatic theater production which, amidst lavish costumes and dance, seeks to touch the deep emotional and moral instincts of the audience.

The Egret Lady

My heart is haunted by love
As the spring moon misted by the cloud.
My covert love engulfs me
Like snow clinging to an umbrella
Impacted against the harsh wind.
I fear, though, my liaison may be ill fated
Not to be fulfilled but to vanish
As the lightest flakes of snow.

In my heart of hearts a darkness reigns.
Look on me with pity in yours.
A lone white egret stands
Bedraggled by the flurries of snow
A mirror image of my misery.

A straying streak of water, thin but firm, it seems annoyed
To have nothing but complaint for unfulfilled affection.

One soon gets used to the pretty pedal playing of the egret
And to our love as well, you say,
Evaporating as a drop of dew?

With no time to wipe my tears
With no time to dry my wet sleeves

I was rushed secretly into your arms
Under the radiant light of the moon.
Our words were lost in oblivion
And I thanked god for our ties.
My joy soared and I did not know
What to do with the glory that suffused me.
How ashamed I was!

How hard it is for me
To see down the pathways of your heart;
As hard as to draw sea water from the Suma beach.
Indeed, indeed.
How hard it is for me to touch and catch your heart;
As hard as it is to crease a satin skirt.
Indeed, indeed!

When the egret's wings flutter flakes of snow whirl down
As the cherry shedding petals.
A precious heap of snow is gone;
But what a touching scene it is.

My sleeve is an umbrella snowed up with cherry petals
As my heart is dyed by my ardent love for my man.
How can I sweep either off?
I can put up a parasol as a good sunshade.
With a lovely parasol let's go to the Yoshino

To see the cherry bloom.
The petals are falling on the wing of parasol.
Twist and twirl the seasons are rolling on
With human knots combined.
Indeed, indeed.
As the knots combine so the rumours spread.

Without having attained my dream to accompany my man,
I lost him torn by the sword miserably amidst a tragic hell
Of cruel conflict here on earth.
A view of the inferno was familiar to me at a glance.

The King of Hell with an iron cane in hand
Questioned the wrong doings of all the people
  dispatched there.
The tortures of the flames were harassing them.
In the scene of carnage, drums were beaten endlessly;
The guards chased me, while I tried to escape,
With iron canes and steel teeth rattling loud behind me
Accusing my straying love.
At last my tiny body was cracked and battered down.

Please accord me some mercy!
The fate of the Egret Lady who lost her virtue for love
And suffered great misery can never be remembered
  without tears.

Combing Black Hair
(Kurokami)
黒髪
Lyrics by Jisuke Sakurada
Music by Sakichi Kineya I

I live in a place called Nira-Yama in Izu peninsula. There is a small historic spot nearby called 'Hiru-ga-Kojima,' where Yoritomo Minamoto, the founder of the Kamakura Dynasty (12th century), was forced to live in confinement between the age of 14 and 34 years old. When captured by Kiyomori Taira, who was in power at the time, young Yoritomo was ordered to be killed along with his brothers. However, because Kiyomori's step-mother took mercy on them and pleaded to save their lives, Yoritomo barely escaped death and was allowed to live in Hiru-ga-Kojima, a small site on the Kano River in Izu. This episode could be interpreted as Kiyomori's fatal error in failing to eradicate the descendants of the Genji family, or it can be supposed that Kiyomori had his own hidden agenda when he made this decision. In either case, Kiyomori's Heike was brought to ruin by the Minamoto brothers decades later.

Yoritomo grew up to be a young man in the scenic surrounding of Nira-Yama. He fell in love with Tatsu-Hime, the daughter of his guardian Sukechika Ito, and through her had a child, Chizu. However, Sukechika, afraid of the wrath of Kiyomori, killed Chizu and forcefully separated Tatsu-Hime from Yoritomo. The lady who consoled Yoritomo's devastated heart was Masako Hojo, the fierce tempered daughter of a powerful local clan. With the support of Tokimasa Hojo, Masako's father, Yoritomo gained enough power to rattle the reins of history, eventually overthrowing the Heike to found the Kamakura Dynasty.

This long historic background is the context in which the short song 'Kurokami' is set (Japanese traditional performing arts, such as Kabuki, typically employ very broad historical contexts). The scene depicted here is Tatsu-Hime combing her long black hair on a silent, dark, snowy night. Her child was murdered and her lover was taken away by Masako. In an abyss of grief, agony and jealousy, she quietly continues to comb her hair, though it must be imagined that her eyes were bloodshot with rage.

This song was written in 1785. Although complex and profoundly dark when its meaning, is properly understood, it is often used as a practice song for beginners including children, because it is a comparatively short piece. These children sing this song not even suspecting the full weight or the harsh realities it describes. However, its pregnant words are etched in their minds like realizations waiting to be born. Thus, it has been noted, maturity dawns all the more quickly to those born into the tradition of Nagauta.

Combing Black Hair

My heart is knotted tight like my black hair tonight
With ever mounting love and jealousy.

Combed was my black hair sleek and silky in your arms.
"Nights of passing fancy" you pretend now. No.
Only a single pillow. What a despair.

Did you not say firm, as if for life 'My love, my wife'?
You have no care
For a woman's feeling in the depths
The hurt when ties are breaking.

Stillness of the sleepless dark:
Can a chink of light be opened
By the temple's morning bell and chase away
My nightmare with the night?

Alas, the flame of grief in love
Flares up in me and graws while dead-white snow
Immures the house in silence
Indifferent to my wakeful sorrow.

A Love Mound in Toba
(Toba no Koizuka)
鳥羽の恋塚
Lyrics by Tosui Nakarai
Music by Kosaburo Yoshizumi

Some Nagauta songs are meant to be used for Kabuki dance performances, while others are composed for the sake of the song itself. 'A Love Mound in Toba' belongs to the latter genre, and is considered as one of the masterpieces among the many of its kind composed from the end of the Edo era until the end of the Meiji.

Nagauta songs are often written to accompany a Kabuki dance, in which case the dance is considered the primary vehicle of expression. These types of songs ('Kanjin-Cho' is a famous example) do not make sense when translated and read outside the context of the dance, since they merely highlight the movements. Songs such as "A Love Mound in Toba," however, have a clear plot development and are suited to translation.

The source of the story is said to be one of the episodes in *Genpei-Josui-Ki* (the tale of war between the Genji and Heike Clans written in the 12th century). A warrior named Morito Endo fell in love with a beautiful lady, Kesa. His violent passion makes him decide to kill Kesa's husband. However, when he sneaks into Kesa's house to kill het husband in the dark, chaste Kesa awaits him in her husband's bed to have her head chopped off instead! The story is bloody and gruesome, yet it ends up with Morito seeing the face of his beloved woman, whom he has just killed, as that of the holy Buddha. As a result of this experience, he later becomes a renowned monk named 'Mongaku-Shonin.'

'Mongaku' was a historically existent monk from the end of the Heian era (mid 12th century) to the beginning of the Kamakura era (early 13th century). It seems he was a person

A Love Mound in Toba

with a very violent temperament. He is said to have killed Kesa, reveled against the retired Emperor Goshirakawa, and when exiled to Izu, encouraged Yoritomo Minamoto to raise an army against the Heike. He was again exiled to Sado and then to Tsushima before finally dying in exile. Assuming from the fact that he was called "a holy ascetic in exile without learning," the actual person was quire different from the figure in the story, whose personality has been beautified through association with the Buddha.

A theme common to many classical Japanese art performances is that of human feelings tragically constrained by old moralistic restrictions. This theme might be called the aesthetic of suppression, and can often be deeply tragic and touching. In many cases reliance on the Buddha and the afterlife is the only hope offered to redeem the characters.

A Love Mound in Toba

A warrior named Morito went to the formal opening
  of a new bridge and saw his lovely cousin lady Kesa
Whose beauty far outshone the cherry blossoms.
Now in now out she was glimpsed through the mist.
She fascinated Morito at first sight. Since then
The snowdrifts of his love for Kesa have been mounting
Day and night half awake and half asleep.

Even such a strong warrior as he
Who could cleave a mountain
Was unable to endure the burden of such a need.
As the season turned,
Spring, full of birdsong on all sides,
Sped by unnoticed.
Summer had arrived
And the chimney of his chest
Was smoldering like a smoky fire against mosquitoes.
His desire as incandescent as the fireflies of high summer
  flared within the hearth of his heart,
Growing fiercely day by day.
How could he tame such turbulence?

Autumn came. His longing for her

A Love Mound in Toba

Became tinted with deeper tones

Of the season's sense of sorrow.

Grasshoppers and crickets scraped their violins all night.

For whom are they yearning?

They must not cry too long,

Lest their tearful voices harass my nerves to fury.

When the dawn came after the long, bitter night,

A couple of geese were seen flying aloof in the sky,

Their touch of serenity powerless to soothe his jealousy.

(Morito)

"Here is your nephew, my aunt!"

(Aunt)

"Indeed, Morito, my nephew!

But why do you look so worn out?

So pitiful and painful!"

Aunt's sleeves were wet with tears.

(Morito)

"Now, my aunt!

Please drop your sentimental words!

Who was it that triggered

This torment hounding me to distraction?

You have turned a potent warrior

Into the ghost of what he was!
I must take my revenge on you!"
Morito grabbed his aunt's neck
And put his sword to her chest.

(Aunt)
"My god, Morito!
Have you lost your senses?
What is the cause of this hatred?
Tell me your detailed story now!"

(Morito)
"I can hardly hold it back!
I truly wanted to marry your daughter, Kesa
And asked you so repeatedly.
But you didn't listen to me, did you?
You never thought anyone could die
Merely of a broken heart.
But my life was virtually snatched
Away by your refusal.
How could I bear to live any more?
My only resource is to take the life of my aunt
Who imposed upon me such bitterness.
Then I will kill myself as well."

A Love Mound in Toba

(Aunt)

"Calm down! Hold hard, my boy!

I confess that I didn't realize

You were so much in love with my daughter.

Now I have a plan to let you meet her tonight."

(Morito)

"You have? Is that true? What a release!

I will come back this evening.

Don't break your promise!"

And he was gone.

(Kesa)

Indeed my existence is so frail.

My attachment to this earth

Is like a tiny mark of moonlight

Lodging in a small drop of dew

Barely clinging to a stalk of grass.

Kesa had decided in her mind to end her life

And to take the eternal journey away from this world

For the sake of her mother and her husband.

She could hardly hold back her tears

But did all she could to subdue them

And accompanied her husband to a banquet

Of moonlight viewing,
Bidding mute farewell to him.

(Wataru, Kesa's husband)
Not having noticed anything,
Wataru urged Kesa to sing
A song attuned to the air of beautiful moonlight
And its hidden chorus of crickets.

   (Kesa)
   "Among all the human partings,
   Those with parents and children
   Are particularly painful
   But nothing is of deeper grief
   Than the parting by death of a married couple.
   My deserted heart, quite at a loss,
   Is staying in the plain of dense grass, and falling
     into a deep abyss.
   Oh! How sad I am!"

(Wataru)
"What kind of ominous tune are you singing?
No bond is firmer than ours!
It is like a pair of birds
Flying together on coordinated wings;

A Love Mound in Toba

Like a pair of trees entwined together
　with all their boughs.
How could a parting be possible?
Let's go to your room and fuse in a sweet dream together.
Oh! How happy I am!"

Wataru stood up joyfully with Kesa.
Kesa hugged him tightly and took him to her room.

Kesa, carefully counting the time as promised,
Quietly crawled out of the bed,
Washed her hair clean and moved into Wataru's bedroom.
Whom was she waiting for?
Not at all for her lover
But for a man stealing in to settle his burning jealousy against
　her husband.
Have mercy on poor Kesa!
She was going to sacrifice herself for her husband
And prove her chastity to him.

Stealthily treading the dews
Of grass in the garden,
Morito reached Wataru's bed.

The moonlight was glowing bright,

But he was blind with the rage of jealous love.

Morito groped and touched wet hair,

It must be Wataru's, as has been plotted, so he thought

And within one stroke beheaded it.

He left the place and turned home with great glee.

Dawn was coming up in a clear sky,

The blizzard of hate was erased.

As he wanted to pray to the Buddha

For the peaceful journey of Wataru

To the Pure Land

He looked again at the severed head.

My god!

It was not Wataru's but the bloody head of Kesa.

What a wild shock it was!

He didn't dare to know whether it was a vision or reality.

He was bitterly stricken with the most horrible awakening.

Suddenly he was enlightened with the thought

That life was in vain after all

As vain as the life of poor Kesa.

Her head, now totally gone pale,

Looked ornamented nobly

With white hairs glowing

At her forehead like the Buddha.

A part of her torn sleeves dyed red with her blood

Even looked like a shred of Buddha's linen

Of mercy guiding people through his heavenly garden.

What a transfiguration!

Morito was touched through and through

With Buddha's mercy

And so he cut off his hair and became one of believers.

After his revelation

Morito changed his name to Moriami

And in later years became the very renowned Priest,

Mongaku, at a temple in Takao.

This is the story of how the Priest Mongaku

Was spiritually awakened.

A mound in Toba where Kesa takes her eternal sleep

  still speaks movingly today to everyone of her tale

Despite the passing of the generations.

House of Tsuna Watanabe

(Watanabe-no-Tsuna no Yakata)

渡辺綱の館

Lyrics taken from a classic Kabuki play
Music by Kangoro Kineya III

This Nagauta was composed in 1869, in the second year of the Meiji era, but the original Kabuki play was said to have been written more than 100 years before that.

A soldier named Tsuna Watanabe, who served Yorimitsu Minamoto (948-1021) encounters an elegantly dressed beauty around Rasho-Mon (Rasho-Gate) in Kyoto at night, and is asked to escort her hack home. As they are riding together on horseback, the beauty reveals herself to be a fierce ogre. Tsuna instantly cuts off one of her arms. The ogre escapes. A Few days later, the ogre comes to Tsuna's house, disguised as his old aunt, to retrieve her lost arm. The main plot of this song is a suspenseful story describing how the ogre enters into Tsuna's house to retrieve her arm. The song is said to be taken from the Tale of Heike. For those interested in the original source of this song, I would recommend reading 'Nagauta-Biiki' by Koichi Ikeda (Sei-A-Boh Publishing Co., 2002). This book also contains information about Tsuna's life and the whereabouts of his grave.

Remember that there was no electricity in those days. The 'darkness' serves as a background to the story, and is the theme of this song. A beautiful woman whom Tsuna comes across in the darkness is an ogre. The arm is cut off with splashes of blood flying into the darkness. Tsuna then abstains himself from worldly contact, and stays alone in his dark house for seven days. The ogre, disguised as an old woman, gradually approaches him, peeps in the box where her arm is kept and gives a gasp: She reveals her true identity, grabs the arm and flies away into the black clouds with a Mephistophelian smile, leaving angerstricken Tsuna behind.

House of Tsuna Watanabe

Tsuna Watanabe, a samurai, sliced off an arm of the Ogre
Whose evil spirit haunted the site of Rashomon
Near Kujou Street, Kyoto,
An exploit that spread his fame and praise
  throughout the town.
But Seimei, the celebrated seer,
Warned him an ogre who lost an arm
Would surely come back and seek revenge
  within seven days.
Tsuna shut himself in his house
  with the doors tightly secured,
Purifying himself ritually the entire allotted seven days
  Reciting the sutra to exorcise all possible mishap
  and the evil eye of the Ogre's revenge.

Sure, it was His Majesty's glory
That spurred on Tsuna to achieve
A feat as brave as lopping off the arm
  of the Ogre haunting Rashomon.
But daring felt a long way off to Tsuna who felt depressed
Confined and hiding in his house to exorcise the Ogre;

When all of a sudden his Aunt arrived from his parental part
  of the country out of the drizzling rain.
With her woven bamboo hat

Sopping and covered in foliage
The stooped old Aunt, deeply moved
By her nephew's exploit had struggled all that way
Leaning on her stick to come at last to Tsuna's house.

The old Aunt stopped at the gate and spoke up
 "It's your Aunt, here I am,
I have come all the way from Settsu!
Please open the gate and let me in!"

A high voice was heard from inside,
"I deeply appreciate your visit
 but I cannot let you into the house,
I am in the middle of purification rituals
In totally unexpected circumstances
And no one must interrupt them."
"What? You won't let me in?"
"No. It can't be helped, dear Aunt."

"What?
Remember it was I who brought you up
And hugged you in your infancy!
During the torrid summer days
I fanned a cool breeze over you.
Through the freezing days of winter,
I warmed you fondly with an extra quilt.
And so it was you grew up

to become fine and manly Tsuna!
Alas, if you don't admit this debt
You can never be recognized as an authentic warrior.
You sound really cruel to talk like this!"
And the Aunt burst into tears.
Having heard her cry even a warrior such as Tsuna
Could not help but obey
And whatever his misgivings opened the gate reluctantly
And led her into his room.

Tsuna bowed obediently and said,
"Please forgive my discourtesy.
Will you share some *'sake'* with me?
  and show me your Noh-dance."

'Sake' restored her temper and enriched the mood
  by her performance opening out like a fan.

"By the way, Tsuna," said his Aunt,
"Where is the arm of the Ogre
You so bravely amputated and
Earned such great renown?"
"Here is the arm, my Aunt."
He opened the Chinese chest
And show her the severed limb within.

She gazed with her eyes half closed,

Trying very hard to scrutinize it for herself.

Her cheeks began to flush

And all of a sudden she seized the arm and swelled up

As her body turned hugely into the Ogre.

His frame burst through the roof

  and towered over the house.

What a terrifying figure the Ogre cut

Glaring around him.

"How dare you, Tsuna,

Imagine you could exorcise

Me, the Ogre Ibaraki-Douji!

Didn't you have the nous to see

I had returned to get my lost arm back?"

Tsuna, transported by rage, roared out of the house and tried

But in vain to slash at the Ogre as he rose up into the sky.

He slashed again and again but the Ogre finally disappeared

Into the dark clouds hemming in the sky.

Tsuna bitterly repented his carelessness

In flouting the advice of the seer, Seimei.

But his eyes were now flaring

With the furious spirit of revenge,

And swore that he would surely behead the Ogre.

Everyone was greatly moved by Tsuna

  in his truly heroic posture.

The Ghoul of the Adachi Plain
(Adachiga-hara no Kijo)
安達ヶ原の鬼女
Lyrics originated from a Noh song
Music by Katsusaburo Kineya II

There was an old legend of a fearful she-ghoul living in the Adachi Plain (situated in Adachi-Gun district in Fukushima Prefecture in the northern part of Japan), who was known to capture humans and devour them. The story was used as the theme of a Noh play, known widely as 'Kuro-Zuka' (literally, Black Mound). This Noh song was again recomposed as Nagauta to be used for Kabuki dance music in the beginning of the Meiji era (1870).

The tradition and culture of Noh thrived under the patronage of feudal lords (Daimyo) throughout the Edo era, but the sudden lack of funding that accompanied the political turmoil of the Meiji Restoration threatened its existence. In a desparate attempt to keep the tradition alive, the Noh establishment decided to appeal to the masses through the induction of Nagauta. 'Adachiga-hara' is a good example of such a case.

The story is as follows: Yukei, a high monk living in Nachi (presently Wakayama Prefecture) went off on a pilgrimage. After a long day's journey, he arrives at the Adachi Plain at nightfall, and is barely able to find a lonely shack where he might lodge for the night. Not realizing that this is the home of the infamous she-ghoul, he asks the old lady who lived there for a night's stay. After getting comfortable and exchanging conversation, the old lady offers to go and get some firewood for the night, and makes the monk promise that he would not look into her room while she is gone. Unable to bear the curiosity, the monk takes a peek, only to find that the room is filled to the ceiling with bones and human remains!

Finally realizing that this was the den of the legendary she-ghoul, Yukei frantically decides to run away. However, the old lady rushes back to the cabin when she notices the commotion. Finding the monk ready to run for his life, she explodes with rage over his broken promise. While she dances in anger, swinging an iron cane, Yukei prays for his life, invoking the deity Fudo-Myo-Oh.

His prayers apparently granted, the she-ghoul's powers wither away, and she is overcome with shame. The sound of distant temple bells finally dispels her completely, and the gripping horror show ends with the ghoul vanishing into thin air.

The Ghoul of the Adachi Plain

(Noh Recitation)

My linen vestment for the trip was wet with drops of dew.

I am the ascetic monk, Yukei of the Tohkoh Temple
  in Nachi

Traveling round the country,

Leading a life in the mountains and seeking sacred places
  such as Kumano

To worship Buddha and escape desires.

(Song)

I had something in my mind to resolve

And so went off on pilgrimage.

From Nachi I passed by Kishu beach,

Hugging beautiful scenes to my heart,

Continued to walk for days and nights

And finally entered the plain of Adachi.

(Yukei)

Alas, the sun set long ago and no village

Has come in sight, only a hut lit by a lantern.

Shall I stop and ask for a night's lodging?

(Old Woman)

Nothing is more desolate than living alone in misery.

Now autumn has settled down upon my life

And floats its chilly air around me in the dawn.
Distress haunts me and I turn
  the leaves of the calendar in vain.
Awake at night
I have to savour every hour of my hopeless life.

Who's that?

(Yukei)
I am a pilgrim and a monk.
Please let me have a night's lodging.

(Old Woman)
How could I allow you to stay
In such a dilapidated, forsaken hut
With the cold wind whistling through?

(Yukei)
Reluctantly, until this hour
  my only pillow has been the grass.
For mercy's *sake*, will you please let me sleep
  in your house?

(Old Woman)
Even for me, this is a cruel hovel,
An awful place to live.

(Yukei)

Please let me in, he shouted

And opened the brushwood gate.

(Old Woman)

Oh! You do look truly miserable!

The woman, emerging from the door, replied.

You may come in and stay with me, my dear.

The monk, refreshing his tired limbs, said

Thank you greatly for your kindness.

(Yukei)

By the way, what is that unusual tool?

(Old Woman)

Oh, that is a reel. It is a tool

For such a poor woman as me to handle.

(Yukei)

Interesting. Please show me how.

(Old Woman)

You make me shy. It embarrasses me

To show you a poor woman's work

As if I lacked a sense of shame.

(Hand-drum Song)

Is it not a deep mercy
  Of the hostess as well
To present moonlight
  Shedding over my bed?
Like the reel winding round
  And bringing
Bright threads again
  In front of me.
Why can't you return
  My good old days?

(Recitation)

Although I have lived long in poverty and misery
I could abandon worldly desires and die
  as a devout Buddhist
Only by observing the way of sincerity.
Life passes in vanities and no one can keep young for long.
Old age catches one anyway in the end.
Complaining against life makes no sense.
It is nothing but a void after all.

(Thread Song)

The noble Hikaru Genji wears a crown
With woven threads hanging as ivy
When he visits his mistress Yugao
  Living near the Gojoh quarter.

A float of Kamo Shrine used
  At the Aoi Festival
Is decorated heavily with lovely threads.

Amid the bloom of weeping cherry blossoms
People gather in the twilight
And praise threads of flowers.

Silver thread grass bears ears in autumn
Longing for the moon to the rise.

The old woman winding the reel before me
Obsessed with the misery of being poor
The whole of her long life,
Never stops keening for the solitude of her longevity,
As plovers wail all night over Akashi Bay.

(Old Woman or Ghoul)
Now, dear Yukei. The chilly drafts are bad for us.
Why don't I go into the bush
  and get some firewood for you?
Please wait a while.

(Yukei)
Thank you for the thought,
But it is late at night and dark outside

And dangerous for a woman.

(Ghoul)
Don't worry about that.
The trails are well known.

(Yukei)
Go, then and see you soon.

(Ghoul)
By the way, Yukei, while I am out
Don't ever look into my room!

(Yukei)
I am no peeping Tom of a monk
Who would peer into your room.

(Ghoul)
Never, mind, never. Agreed?

(Yukei)
I swear.

Heaven help us.
The monk looked into the room through the crevice
  and found
Countless human remains piled up to the ceiling.

The Ghoul of the Adachi Plain

Bloody pus was flowing out of the bodies.
Skins and flesh were raw and rotting.
The room was filled with an appalling stench.

Now he knew what this was the den of the famous ghoul
Said to hide in the Black Mound area
   of the plain called Adachi.

My God, how frightening! how terrifying!
This really was the hide-out of the ghoul, her den!

Beside himself with fear, the monk rushed out of the hut with
   no idea where to go.

(Ghoul)
Wait, monk! You broke your promise
   and exposed my room.
That's why I'm rushing back in rage.
The flame of my anger burns
My soul through and through
As if a fire storm had incinerated
The palace of an ancient Chinese Emperor.
Wind blows in the plain
And thunder and lightening
Filled the universe through the mountain:
Clouds whirled jet-black with heavy rain.
The ghoul flung her iron cane around

And tried to devour the monk, with a furious power!

(Prayer)
"May I address my prayer to you,
Fudo-Myo-oh, the Protector.
When I behold you my spirit awakes again.
I summon the energy to will the good
And vanish all the evils.
I beseech you to confer great wisdom on me
And liberate me from helplessness."

By the grace of the threads
Gathered up in the hand of Fudo-Myo-oh,
Yukei prayed hard
In face of the ghoul and tortured her out of him.

The Ghoul was totally exorcised;
Her hide-out was exposed.
Once her anger flaring fiercely had leaked away
Tottering around as in a trance.

"Oh the shame of my shape."
She groaned with a dreadful voice,
And finally faded in the dark
At the sound of the temple bell.

Frog
(Kawazu)

蛙

Lyrics by Soan Takahashi
Music by Jokan Kineya

The lyric of this fairly short piece was written by Soan in the 3rd year of Showa (1928). Soan was a journalist, a director for a large company, and a master of tea ceremony, renowned for his refined taste. He is said to have had a wide acquaintance with the business leaders of the time, and also wrote other elegant lyrics such as '*Sake*,' 'Warai (laughter),' and 'Chikara (strength).' Music for those lyrics were composed by Jokan Kineya, who was famous for being the undisputed master of the *shamisen* instrument. Those lyrics are now a precious relic of the bygone Taisho era, when extravagant pleasures were enjoyed by the refined wealthy people of the time.

Although short, the music is said to be laden with hidden themes, which may only be recognized by those knowledgeable about Nagauta. The lyric is scattered like a mosaic with many legends and famous names of literary figures. This Nagauta is likened to a soothing breath of fresh air.

Frog

An ancient poet, a name to conjure with,

Kino-Tsurayuki cited

Frog in the preface of a famous anthology

The Kokin-Waka

As one of the two most frequently

Recurring characters in it.

Frog can truly bask in the honor

Of recognition from such a source.

Frog's charm has attracted ever so many in the past

And attracts ever so many today

Because he offers splendid topics

For life histories in such abundance.

The master calligrapher Ono-Tofuh

Learned much for his art

Watching a frog leap again and again,

And again to land on a high willow bough.

It led Ono-Tofuh to a revelation

Of the hard and narrow road, the training

That finally made of him a Master.

The great Haiku poet, Matsuo-Bashou,

Listening to the sound of a frog
Jumping into a quiet pond,
Was initiated into the deep Zen state
Of distilled and meditative solitude
That finally made of him a Master.

An old story tells us a frog living in Kyoto
Went on a journey to Osaka.
On his way at the pass of Hora
For the first time he saw
Osaka beneath him.
Deeply disappointed, he murmured
'But Osaka is no different from Kyoto!'
And turned home in rare dejection.

Silly frog! He did not realize
His eyes could only see what lay behind him.

This year is indeed an auspicious one.
Dear frogs, my lovely friends!
Put on your handsomest frog coat and kneel
Prettily with your palms to the ground,
Bow low before your party lords and masters.
And a juicy gratuity will be granted you!

Frog

(Resting Song)

"Isn't this the famous fun-loving Asakusa area?
Lucky frog contrived to sneak successfully
Into the backyard of Yoshiwara,
The grand and exclusive red lantern place
But a heartless thunderstorm soaked him through
And sent him scuttling across the paddy."

Extreme caution was required.

Watch out for dangerous serpents!

If one should find him

Discretion would be the order of the day

Help! Help!

Frog ran into the undergrowth of leaves

To hide away.

A Puppeteer
(Kairaishi)
傀儡師
Lyrics by an anonymous writer
Music by Saburosuke Kineya IV

A Puppeteer

This song dates back to around 1830, though its subject, the 'street puppeteers,' appeared in Japan as early as the Heian era (8th to 12th century). In those days, puppeteers wandered the country in hopes of making enough change to support their wife and children waiting in the country village. These wandering artists with weathered skin and raspy voices would walk from town to town carrying a large puppet box on their back, hoping for some voice or another to call them into their home for a show. Then, to the popular tunes of the day, the puppeteer blows life and dance into his puppets. A dream world unfolds between the puppet and his master, the puppeteer. Between the life-like dance of the puppet and the songs of the puppeteer's wandering life on the road, the boundary between dream and reality dissolves. In this song, the dream world evoked by the puppeteer is likened to mountain cherries in full bloom on Mt. Yoshino... an image of both beauty and transience, since the blossoms last for only a short while. The performance ends with the puppeteer's praise to this fleeting and beautiful life, and his thanks for the opportunity to make his day's wage.

The puppets are then packed back in their box and reduced to lifelessness. This image of a sedate ending following the short and beautiful dance of life is truly in accord with the Japanese spirit and aesthetic.

A Puppeteer

Here I am, a Puppeteer,

Seeking a livelihood in this harsh world

Scouring the country never at home

From the sunset shore of the west

To the Shogun's capital,

Kamakura, in the east unattended, without company.

Lanes of willows sprout new shoots

And mingle with camellia blooms

All dripping from spring rain.

So is my hood but my tread lightens as it nears a city

Gentle accents, floating through a window

And across a sumptuous gate, seduced me,

  stop me in my tracks;

"Puppeteer! I want to see them dancing!"

Oh yes, you may! You may!

Tapping out a rhythm on the doll's case

He extracts a chain of lovely puppets

And intones "Dance, dance!"

A kind of chanting in a husky voice,

As they weave their steps with a naive charm.

A Puppeteer

I sprang up as a solitary blade of grass

Waving in a country plain.

As time goes by, other ears emerged

When tufts of love piled up

And made the thousand dew drops jealous of me!

But now,

I travel and I lodge alone

Spending night hours by myself

As long as the lynx tail shadows.

My sweetest wife, tender as a bride

Taken the night before, handles a sickle gracefully.

Oh she is lovely. She attracts everyone around her.

I hide my gratified blushes and cannot help adoring

Her skill in sewing and weaving

Golden and silver threads tight

Into robes of radiance

As if the nocturnal pillow whispers

Only for the two of us.

No wonder I am blessed with three sons.

The eldest is a sulky fellow folding his arms and mouth shut

Even before his father.

The second is just a lanky boy.

The last one is really lovable

Six or seven years old a little rascal of mischief.

I took him on my shoulders to the sites in the capital
With a pin wheel, paper toys and a drum
Grasped tightly in his tiny hands.

If you wish, why not visit Yoshino
The mountain buried under cherry blossom?
Yoshino in full bloom!
Sightseers in endless files trip by treading cheerfully on air,
Their gala dresses and their hats
  snowed under with new fallen petals.

Even servants with canteens in their sleeves,
Wear fancy dresses with jade beads.

Fickle as the spring, blue sky now turns to leaden cloud
Reflecting subtly on the blossoms.
The long lines linger on
Clutching colourful offerings for the shrines
And slowly blur into the twilight.
How joyful life is in this reign!

And with those words, the puppeteer suspends the dolls.
Their dance is done.
Helplessly, they bunk down in their case again.

Lion Dance in Echigo
(Echigo no Shishi-Mai)
越後の獅子舞い
Lyrics by Kinji Shinoda
Music by Rokuzaemon Kineya IX

This Nagauta was first composed in 1812 for a Kabuki dance, and is based on a local folk dance originating from the Echigo (present Niigata Prefecture) region. 'Lion Dance in Echigo' is the synonym of 'Kakubei Jishi (Kakubei Lion).' Kakubei Jishi dancers were street performers who danced with Japanese mythical lion masks. 'Kakubei' is a man's name, but it is not clear whether it was the name of someone who carved these wooden masks, or the name of the head of the dance troupe who first brought the dance into vogue. I prefer to assume that Kakubei was a talented man who sculpted lion masks and used them to dance and entertain people.

These lion masks are quite dramatic, and have traces of Chinese glamor. Along with the masks, the fancy dance costumes, the adorable child dancers and accompanying drum and flute music, all make for an exquisite show. However, there is also a certain pathos inherent in the performance, for it is understood that these street dancers had to leave their families to wander around the country to earn their living. It is this contrast between the brilliant external appearance and a certain inherent sadness that is responsible for the enduring popularity of this song.

Another point of interest is that a 'lion song' sung in Echigo dialect is praised in the lyric to possess 'a special charm.' Indeed, any classic folklore proves more effective when recited in its own dialect, reflecting its local characteristics.

Lion Dance in Echigo

Drums are beaten in the lucid air.

The Lion Dance has come to town

With shouts advertizing

"Kakubei! Kakubei!"

The famous choreographer and lion-head sculptor.

The people press in crowds all agog

To see the floral lion dance and hear

The legend of the Stone Bridge,

Where a monk met a woodcutter who later turned into a lion

Faithfully dancing for the monk.

Although I hope the show

Appears to have effortless grace

I have to work at it constantly.

I do all the singing and the dancing

And the accompaniment myself, without an aide.

When evening comes, I sleep alone

With only the grass for a pillow.

I am too reticent to talk about my wife,

My dream companion every night

Who is so talented a cook so deft at all kitchen work.

I can't help but smile to myself

When I bask in my memories of her
Cuddling up to me insinuatingly.

Among many good things in Echigo
The lion dance sung in the local dialect
Is indeed a special show.
When autumn comes and rabbits turn white
I wish I could ask a flying goose
To carry my letter to convey this
With a souvenir of fine crepe for her.

Formerly I thought I was like a brother to her
  but now I am her man
Since our knot has been closely tied.

(Beach Song)
Is he coming soon? Is he coming?
I walk to the beech and wait.
The moan of the wind through the pines
Pierces my heart.
  "Yatto-kukeno. Oh
The cold wind of the pines."

Daffodils are falling in love
The very willows are being chased.

But the longing roused
As the summer flowers bloom
Haunt us in autumn foliage.
  "Yatto-kakeno. Oh
The bitterness of waiting."

Why not forget the bitterness?
Let us sing the '*Okesa*' song together.
There is no point in repining.

The ritual of the lion dance is like a gorgeous peony
Even without a canopy of flowers.
Let me put on my big lion head and dance around the yard
My whole body stamping out the rhythm.

When girls and their siren voices
In chorus enhance my dance with the vivid sound of the
  '*Okesa*' song
Why don't you have a good time with me?
I could wait all night.
I say "Come to me, let's talk" and take her
  to the shade of the pine
To exchange our tender endearments
  in the afterglow of the lion dance.

On the veranda of the house at the hillside opposite
A seventeen-year-old girl drowsily luxuriates
  in a midday nap
Worn out from the hard work
  of lopping off bamboo branches.
Is she not dreaming of enticements
  in her ripe young womanhood?

Now look at the huge crowd!
Stretching from west to east
  all the seats are filled with them.
The throng is like a mountain range
  or the multitudinous waves of the sea,
An endless scarf men and women, white horses on the river.

Let's wind up now,
Whatever the joy of performance has been today
  just as one rolls up all the long strips
  of bleached cloths out of the stream
And let's go home!

The Opulence of Kinokuni-ya
(Kibun Daijin)
紀文大尽―紀伊国屋文左衛門の豪遊―
Lyrics by Choji Nakauchi
Music by Rokushiro Kineya and
Kosaburo Yoshizumi

Bunzaemon Kinokuniya I (Ki-Bun) is said to be a true historical figure in the late 17th century. No written record is left about this man, though his legend as a charismatic businessman and millionaire was solidified and spread after his death. He is known today as a man born in Kishu (present Wakayama Prefecture), who eventually built his fortune by sailing on stormy seas at the risk of his own life in order to deliver oranges to Edo (Tokyo). It is a story not unlike the rich adventurer/tradesman stories of Phoenicia.

The story of Bunzaemon, however, does not end there. It goes on to describe his son, Bunzaemon II, who was deeply spoiled by his father's vast fortune. Critics may argue as the lazy son, brought up in the utmost luxury, who spent his life frittering away his father's fortune to play day and night in the Yoshiwara red-light district. However, I myself imagine he had no choice but to live like this, and feel empathy for his unfortunate destiny. Had he continued to increase his inherited fortune, he would have incited jealousy among his competitors, and might well have been killed! His reckless spending may have been the only road left by the grim reaper, ever present amidst the glitter of his gold.

This long story is divided into two parts. The first half is the story of the bravery and success of Ki-Bun I, the father, and of the emerging nihilism and decadence of his son, Ki-Bun II. The second half highlights some of the episodes from Ki-Bun II's life, such as his spreading of gold coins over the snow-scape of the tea house garden, and of the preachy lecture about true love that he receives from a red-light district entertainer.

Ki-Bun's luxuries described towards the end of the lyric go beyond splendor, verging on an decadent and destructive aestheticism. Yet even this pitiful vanity became beautified over time, and the legend of the Ki-Bun I and II became attributed with typical Japanese characteristics worthy of fondness and admiration.

The Opulence of Kinokuni-ya

(Sailors' Song)

We never fear even the roughest sailing

Off Hachijou Island far from land

Which birds themselves can hardly reach,

But how are our loving wives and kids

To bear up, left behind at home?

Rowing and rowing many days and nights

Without sleep, they have finally arrived

At the beach of their determination.

Ahoy! Ahoy! Now everyone is merry.

(Narrative)

It was in the mid-seventeenth century

And in early November

When continued storms whirled the sea.

No ships nor even birds could master their fury

But the boat of Kinokuni-ya

Defied the ocean in the face of the wind.

Let it smash the mast and the sail!

The daredevil sailors rowed the boat unaided

Shouting, Esshi! Esshi!

Daring death in their coffin clothes

Ready even for the worst scenario
Their sleeves tucked up to wage the fight.
At last they overcame the worst of the storm
And rounded the point into Tokyo Bay
Heaving to off Shinagawa.
The boat they brought in with a full load of oranges
Was known to all as the Devil's Ship.

They unloaded and transported
Eighty five thousand baskets of oranges
On eight hundred and fifty carts
As if their lives depended on it to the Kanda fruit market.
It was the Festival of Bellows
And all the local merchants needed oranges
  for the celebrations
Having run short because of storms.
Kinokuni-ya hit the market!
He made a fortune! Fifty thousand Ryou,
Gorgeous flowers of gold.
His business flowered as fruitfully.
It was the founding of the merchant empire
  of Kinokuni-ya the First.

(Dream Sequence)
Yoshiwara, the red-light district, disdainful of a night

That brings on darkness glows like a radiant Palace

  of Taishaku-Ten,

The guardian angel of Buddha's truth

Decorated with endless shining treasures.

Oblivious to the falling of night

And the visitation of dawn,

He repeatedly exchanged cups

Of *sake* with lady entertainers

Until tired at last of intoxication

Saturated with worldly desires.

He dozed off by a footwarmer under a quilt cover

And in the early morning as the snow fell

His father appeared to him in a dream

Emblematic of the tie between father and son.

(Dialogue with lady entertainer, Kichou)

"Dearest love, are you all right?"

Feeling her gentle touch on his back, he opened his eyes.

"Oh, it's you, Kichou, my love.

Though it warms the heart to recall old days of hope,

I am ashamed of what I have made of my luck.

Life indeed is unpredictable.

My father built up a fortune for me to throw away.

Father's last words to me were:

Life offers one chance only to anyone

But his reputation can outlast a man for generations.

It doesn't matter if he makes a fortune or if he spends it

But it does matter that his fame

Should last in the minds of people as a model to be admired.

If they long remember the name of Kinokuni-ya

My heart's desire will be fulfilled.

My ambition shall be satisfied.

My father left these words and died.

And here I am. life is a vacant dream.

Love? Vanity? What does either mean?"

(Kichou)

"No, dear heart, I don't think so.

I believe in true love.

If I sincerely love someone

I still have to serve others to survive.

I bear this real burden and endure.

If you doubt the true love of courtesan

You are too absolute and extreme

And, as a reasonable man,

Should not utter such cruel words.

Truth and falsehood in affairs should arise

From the same source of passionate sincerity.

Even if relations start out as true love

And she is devoted to him with all her heart,

The Opulence of Kinokuni-ya

Even being willing to die with him,

Her sincerity will not reach him

If their encounters become scarce,

The river of the Milky Way will be filled with white horses

And the love lanes trampled under hoof.

When she is redeemed by someone as wife or concubine

The old oath of love may be abandoned.

And yet what started out only as an affair

  without any serious affection

May turn into the real thing if the encounters are repeated:

Frequent ties cultivate true love."

(Kinokuni-ya, Jr.)

Our ties are neither tight nor loose......

The fellow Itchou, the male entertainer,

  sang a song only yesterday...... let me recall it:

  My old straw hat

  Has long been frayed

  Even the strings have been torn off.

  But I never care to replace it

  Nor abandon it either......

Hey! Aren't you Nishubann Kichibei?

Is it true that Naramo, that rascal,

123

Is having a loud party of snow viewing there
  at the far end of the garden
And that it's high time to join the fun?

(Kichibei)
Yes, Sir.

(Kinokuni-ya, Jr.)
What a laugh if I got rid of the snow and gave him a shock!
That would really be living it up!
Do you follow me, Kichibei?

(Kichibei)
Certainly, Sir!

Kichibei knowing what the effect would be
Prepared three hundred Ryo coins of pure gold
And scattered them over the garden, shouting
"Golden rain is falling!".
All the men and women in the house
Rushed out of the room and scrambled and tumbled
After the gold coins as bees after honey.
The scene of pure white snow
Became a mud swamp in the shambles.

The Opulence of Kinokuni-ya

(Dancing Song)

Look out to sea and far away!
Even in the early morning darkness
You will catch white sails.
Yes, those are the Satsuma boats
Of Kinokuni, Kinokuni!

Have you ever been to his fabulous parties?
Setting aside the gorgeous ones thrown in Korea and China
For our party-lovers there's nothing
To match the opulence of Kinokuni-ya.
The beautiful Kichou was redeemed
By Kinokuni-ya, a perfect balance
Of her beauty and his wealth.
He even presented to the owner
Of the goodwill vested in the name of Kichou
Such a fortune in silk cloths
And so splendid a sword.
The man's future was assured.
Let us recall all those glittering feasts so brilliant,
  so out of this world,
So dizzy in dazzling flamboyance!
Let's record this celebratory lyric
For the fame of Kinokuni-ya!

Utsubozaru—*The Monkey and the Quiver*
(Utsubozaru)
靭猿
Lyrics originated from Kyogen
Music by Katsusaburo Kineya

Utsubozaru—*The Monkey and the Quiver*

Originally, "Utsubozaru" was one of the classic comedy plays (Kyogen) performed between Noh performances. It was developed into a dance performance in the beginning of 19th century, and is said to have been rewritten as a Nagauta in 1869.

A feudal lord goes hunting in the fields on a spring day and sees a show-man with a beautiful little monkey. Upon seeing this, the lord, who had been looking for a fur cover for his quiver, wants the monkey's fur.

The lord sends his servant (Taro-Kaja) to the show-man to ask for the monkey's fur, but the show-man pleads for the monkey's life, saying his own humble living depends entirely on the performance of the little monkey. Abusing his authority, the lord even tries to shoot the monkey with an arrow. Abandoning any hope to save the monkey's life, the show-man then says that he will kill the monkey himself by a single blow of a club, so that the monkey's fur is not blemished with an arrow.

Overwhelmed by emotions, the show-man tells the monkey that he is disgusted with himself to have to kill it after he raised it with such care from the time that it was born, but that he cannot disobey the lord's order. He asks the monkey for forgiveness, and not to hold a grudge against him.

When the show-man raises his club for the final blow, the monkey misunderstands it as a signal to start a performance and begins to dance. Seeing this, the show-man once again asks the lord's mercy on the poor monkey.

Touched by this incident, the lord then releases the animal. The show-man lets the monkey perform the last dance before leaving the place in a hurry. The day approaches its end, and in the sky a flock of wild geese heads for the north, far above the fully blossoming cherry trees.

All are gone, and what is left is the quiet and beautiful scenery of the Sumida River at dusk, with the distant view of Mount Fuji and the mountains of Tsukuba.

This is a very elegant piece of Nagauta which leaves a pleasant aftertaste.

Utsubozaru—*The Monkey and the Quiver*

The art of archery arose when the Gods walked the earth.

The quiver containing the arrows was called Utsubo

From its resemblance, being covered with fur,

To Utsubo, the staple hood the ear of millet,

Or so they say.

The monkey of monkeys was the hyperactive Son-Go-Kuh,

Famous in Chinese legend for growing out of a stone egg

Discharged when a giant rock burst open.

(Song of Seasons)

Autumn wind carries the sound of a horn

Played by a resting mower: an ambiguous sound,

But it turned out to be the deer calling for its mate.

Their love was obstructed by the brook in the valley

Where a red rain of maple leaves battered by the showers

Was scattered all over the trails.

Now that the winter is gone with the melting snows

Tangled worries may also depart,

My heart be swollen with expectancy

In the remnants of the snow.

Utsubozaru—The Monkey and the Quiver

The spring is on its way and the banquet of flowers
Is a feast of excitement and delight!
Lords and even their servants get drunk on the melodies
Of endless *Shamisen* playing.
Intoxicated eyes reach far to the banks of the river Sumida
Weighed down with cherry blossom.
A ferry approached the shore plying his trade with shouts of
'Take-ya! Take-ya!'.
Among the crowd of passengers
There alighted a traveling showman
With a pet monkey on his shoulder.

(Dialogue)

(A Lord)

"Taro-Kaja, where are you?"

(Servant)

"At your side, my lord."

(Lord)

"Ask the showman
Where he is taking that monkey on his back."

(Servant)

"Hey there, monkey showman,
Where are you taking your monkey?"

Prostrating himself with his hands on the ground
The traveler said:
"I am a monkey showman
Living in these parts. I am calling on
My clients as I do every day.
Please excuse us, for I am in a hurry…"

(Servant)
"One moment, monkey showman.
That gentleman is a Lord of reputation.
He has taken a spring field trip
  for hunting game with his bow.
He has been searching a long time
For some handsome fur to cover his quiver.
Now, at last, with luck, he has found one!
It is his strong desire to ask of you that you offer him
Your monkey's fur!"

(Showman)
The showman was astounded and appalled.
"How can the Lord want my monkey's fur?
How could I offer the Lord the fur of a live monkey?

I depend every day of the year

On the good will of my monkey.

If I sacrifice his life to the Lord

I will lose both him and my living.

I beg the Lord his pardon and that he will excuse me

  this disaster."

(Lord)

The Lord, paying no heed to the showman's plea for pardon,

Was about to shoot the animal with his bow

In his high-handed lordly way.

(Showman)

"Wait, please wait a minute.

If you shoot the monkey to acquire his fur,

The fur itself will be damaged by the wound.

I know the monkey's vital spot.

Leave this to me instead."

(Servant)

Taro-Kaja agreed but gave him no respite

Urging him on: "Hurry up! Be quick!"

(Showman)

"My poor monkey! Listen carefully.

The request of this Lord is dreadful, in fact intolerable.

But how can I disobey?

I who reared you as a baby have to end up

Doing such a terrible thing to you.

How miserable I am, too!

Now I have to give you a blow.

Please do not bear a grudge against me

And haunt me from the grave…"

The showman, resigned to his fate,

Raised the cane over his head.

But what a scene ensued!

The monkey suddenly began

To dance fiercely beneath the cane.

How touching it was!

"Oh my! Just look at him.

He has no idea the cane was raised to strike him

And plays a trick of rowing a boat!"

(Lord)

"What?

The monkey runs through his mime

Without the slightest idea he might be killed.

How touching! How moving!

Taro-Kaja!

Tell the showman not to strike him!

I say, not to strike him!

Tell him to take his monkey back home!"

The showman was beside himself

With relief and utterly thankful to the Lord.

Kneeling before him,

He said in ringing tones:

"In return for your courteous pardon

I will get the monkey to dance."

(Dance)

"Behold! Monkey is the sacred envoy of the San-noh Shrine.

Let him dedicate a joyous Noh-dance

To celebrate the prosperity of your fief."

Good fortune rains down from heaven

In gorgeous clothes and brocades.

Golden flowers are biooming on earth.

What a fertile age it is!

(Showman)

"Now let us bid farewell,"

Said the showman to the monkey

And turned back on his way.

Geese remote in the sky are heading back north,
Leaving behind the cherry blossom in bloom.
Mountain views of Fuji and Tsukuba
Rise on the horizon
And the air of spring twilight hangs over the stream
Of the River Sumida.

Evergreen Pine
(Matsu no Midori)

松の緑

Lyrics and Music by
Rokusaburo Kineya IV

It is said that those who like fishing have an inevitable fondness for carp fishing, which is thought incomparable to any other type of fishing. Indeed, the zest of fishing is said to start and end with carp fishing.

This Nagauta may then be likened to carp fishing, in the sense that it is one of the first songs that beginners practice, yet it is also a song that professional Nagauta singers long to master. In other words, the path of Nagauta begins with 'Matsu no Midori', and also ends with 'Matsu no Midori.'

Previously I had misunderstood this song to be about the celebration of a daughter's wedding, and was wondering why a young innocent girl was portrayed as a 'pleasure lady' or entertainer. However, I later came to understand that the sting was actually about the new name given to the girl by her master for accomplishing a certain level in art, and then understood why such a metaphor was used.

The song is said to have been composed in the 1850s, just before the Meiji era was to start. The atmosphere at the apex of Edo culture, in all its maturity, is well expressed through the rich ambience of a red light district.

Although the song is only about eight minutes long (the reason why it is suitable for beginners), it is an elaborate piece with rich context and a precise structure. The ultimate merit to use this song for beginners' practice may lie in the fact that, in later years when they listen to it again, the song should certainly remind them of their kind but strict teacher who had taught them so attentively. The solemn ripening depicting a pine tree is meant to trigger the memory of the singer's first Nagauta teacher, who would remain as fresh as an evergreen pine tree in the singer's heart.

Evergreen Pine

With each cuckoo call of spring
The clustering needles of the pine
Grow thicker and greener, year on year
Perhaps for a thousand yet to come.

Even as a fresh shoot this young girl emanates
A charm that casts before her the prime aura
Of what will one day be a great court lady.

Celebrate her restraint and poise
As she treads the ground with patterned steps
Perfectly balanced on her high-soled sandals
And deploys the liquid fringes of her skirt!
No creature could be gifted with a greater grace.
The compound waiting for her, ringed around
By ancient pines with robust roots
Swelling firmly from the ground,
Will be a new world made to measure for her.
Little by little, peering through the hedge,
She will assess the world, its virtues and its vices,
Little by little, she will grow and graduate
From today's slip of a girl with a girl's coiffure
And trace maturely into silver age

The path of life ordained by fortune.

Towards the fulfillment of your heavenly destiny
May you grow through long and flourishing years.
Let us raise our cups to an ever green life
That broadens out in every branch to wisdom!

The Tale of the Seawater Drawers of Suma Beach
(Shiokumi)
汐汲み

Originated from a Noh song
Lyrics by Jisuke Sakurada II
Music by Shojiro Kineya II

Suma beach, located to the west of Kobe overlooking Awaji island on the other side of the Seto Inland Sea, is historically noted for its beauty. Brought up in Kobe, I have a favorable impression of Suma, and even admire the people who live there for the refined taste I imagine they must possess.

This song is rooted in an old legend. Yukihira Ariwara, the elder brother of Narihira Ariwara, the famous waka-poet of the Heian era renowned for his talent and beauty, was exiled from Kyoto to Suma. There he met the beautiful sisters 'Matsu-kaze (pine wind)' and 'Mura-same (passing rain),' who were hiding from their spiteful stepmother and making their living as salt makers. Yukihira sympathizes with them and eventually falls in love with Matsu-kaze, spending a joyous three years with them on Suma Beach.

However, after returning to Kyoto, Yukihira never got in touch with the sisters again, though the sisters waited patiently for him to return. After a while, they heard the news of Yukihira's death, and thereafter lived their life in solitude, remembering Yukihira by the hat and hunting cloak he left as a memento.

There is also a Noh song called 'Matsu-kaze' derived from the same legend. The story is about a travelling monk's encounter with the ghosts of the sisters on Suma beach. The ghosts, still obsessed with love for Yukihira, dance gracefully on the beach wearing Yukihira's hat and cloak, and the monk is asked to pray for the salvation of their spirit. When the dawn comes, the monk finds himself alone on the beach with only the sound of the wind and crying of birds, and realizes he was dreaming. The obsession of love is beautiful, yet also fragile, hollow, and maddening. After the ghosts disappear in the first light of day, only the quiet beach is left surrounded by the profound calm of immortality.

Unlike in Noh, Matsu-kaze and Mura-same are not depicted as ghosts in this Nagauta. Although the atmosphere of Kabuki and Nagauta is more baroque than the Noh, the two songs both aim to express the elegance of the Japanese aesthetic.

The Tale of the Seawater Drawers of Suma Beach

The firm old pine tree on the beach
With its spreading roots and evergreen needles
Always brings to mind the handsome nobleman
Yukihira Ariwara
Hanging his usual hat and hunting cloak.
Ejima of Awaji Island
From the shore opposite Suma beach
Despatches white horses to the strand
But conveys no tender messages
From the lover to the lonely sisters
Who wait so patiently in vain.

Even these poor hard-working women
Busy day after day on the shore
Cannot bear the empty life without him
And wet their sleeves with tears.
Is there no one to tell him
Ever to join them in joyful reunion?
Always dreaming of his return
They labour at drawing seawater.

"Look"
Matsu-kaze, an elder sister sighed with grief,
"When I pour water into the two tubs

The moon sits equally in each.

One moon creating two moon images.

The third moon, ah, is beyond the clouds.

My love, you are unreachable indeed."

Is this area called Naruo?

Let me rest at the foot of the pine

Sensing serene moonlight on my back.

As always

How beautiful the evening scene is.

Fishermen awake the waters

Calling one another with voices

That give even seagulls a sharp jolt

And send them scattering,

As mischievous gossip spreads

Like the smoke that billows from the chimneys

Of the salt drying ovens along the beach.

Who cares!

Three years explored the lusts

Of enchanted rendezvous.

No news was heard from Yukihira

For whom I still wait at Suma beach

Stopping often at the old pine

That holds such potent memories

In hopes of finding him at home.

His hunting cloak as a memento

Haunts regret like bitterness.

On the night of our first encounter
I was so ardent
I hardly cast away my sash.
We lay down covered by his hunting cloak
And whispered words of love
With passionate promises for the future.

My darling, how is such a beautiful bird
Singing for me?
With a sad call that will not fly away?
A trill of wishes for our reunion?

I shall always wait for you and long
And so there will be no time
To dim the force of our commitment.

Since that first night our bonding as two lovers
Has sealed up watertight.

(Umbrella Dance)
Here's an umbrella for you
Wet with the rain of love.
Take a sedge hat to avoid prying eyes
Or an umbrella of sky-blue wishes

Counting the days to the next encounter.
How bitterly hard it is to be kept waiting as long
As the long handle of an umbrella!
Use a parasol for an uneasy time.
Present a lordly man wearing a white hunting cloak
A long sheath for umbrella and show him your fidelity.
Use one umbrella for the two hugging close in love.
If I were named as your true wife
What a special hat I would acquire.
What a lovely hat I would have
With gorgeous flowers around the brim!

The dragging sounds of waves touched my heart
As I bade farewell and walked away.
Though I thought I heard a sound of rain falling
Over the Suma beach in the night,
I know once the dawn appeared
Only the soughing of the wind
Came through the pine trees standing there ……

The solitary drawer `Matsu-kaze'
Or 'Pine wind'
Waiting for her lordly lover in vain
Left a melancholy story behind
A legend for generations.

Willow Trees on the Bank
(Kishi no Yanagi)
岸の柳
Lyrics by an anonymous writer
Music by Shojiro Kineya III

In 1868 (4th year of Keio), just before the Meiji Restoration took place, the reformists' army calling for the end to the shogunate's reign at the last moment suspended their attack on Edo city (Tokyo) as a result of a thoughtful negotiation between Takamori Saigo, the leader of the army, and Kaishu Katsu of the shogunate government. In a truly ideal end to the fierce political strife, the Edo castle was surrendered to the opposing army without bloodshed, and Edo escaped the flames of war. In 1871 (4th year of Meiji), the same Takamori Saigo was given the important mission of subduing the remaining resistance forces, and of restoring peace and order after the political confusion of the Restoration. My grandfather was born in 1867 (3rd year of Keio), so the story does not sound like an ancient episode to me.

This Nagauta was composed in 1873 (6th year of Meiji). The poem is about the refined atmosphere of high-class Japanese restaurants (ryoutei) in the famous Yanagi-Bashi district on the bank of the Sumida River. When we think of the messy historical background to this period, it is almost a miracle that the refined world of entertainment represented by the 'ryoutei' managed to survive due to the governance efforts of Takamori Saigo, who himself is said to have been a man of honest poverty against corrupted new rulers of the early Meiji era.

It is difficult to imagine that the Edo-style refinement described in this song existed at a time of such political turmoil. In any case, it is a scene of beauty and splendor worthy of a heartfelt offering to Takamori Saigo, to whom its conservation is indebted.

Willow Trees on the Bank

The light of summer on Mt. Tsukuba
Looked as fresh as the hostesses
In their billowing yukata.
Their moist black hair glittered in the breeze
And their almond eyes under the pencilled brows
Curving to sharp ends like willow leaves
Enticed us on.
My heart beat fast as my small ferry
Approached the pier
Where the pleasure boat was moored
On which the beauties waited.

A lively tune was already being plucked
On the *shamisen*.
To whom were those willow leaves attuned?
The breeze was in step with the melody.

My ardent desires were on the brink of being tested
For now the ferry oars made contact with the bank.
Through the screens of the windows of the boat
Shadows of lively women played.
They were chanting songs with the first corners
In happy harmony like practised choir.

Does playing like this presage a new love?
Such frivolous nonsense almost gives one hope!

White horses of the river lurching forward and held back
Sound like a hail of hand drums,
The pattern of swollen waves recalls
Traditional Japanese art designs.
With all these images you could feel yourself
Attending an original Biwa performance.

You may dream of cruising on lake Biwa
While the glitter of ethereal nymphs,
Attendants of the lovely Benzai goddess
Shines down on the surface of the lake
And their dance revolves to the serene airs
Of *koto* notes and flutes floating through space.

As you look to the further horizon
There stands the shrine of grace, Ben-Zai-Ten.
Wave upon wave of people are walking endlessly
Across the bridge to reach that grail.
It's like a rainbow lane offered by the goddess
Helping a hand to the people of this world
Longing for a better life through the joy of song.

Benkei on Board
(Funa Benkei)
船弁慶
Lyrics originated from a Noh song
Music by Katsusaburo Kineya II

This Nagauta is a masterpiece written by Mokuami Kawatake (1816-1893), a famous Kabuki playwright who flourished in the beginning of the Meiji era. Like many Nagauta and Kabuki plays, it has its origin in the Noh play under the same name.

Yoshitsune Minamoto, the tragic prince of the Genji clan who seized power in the late 12th century, had served with distinction assisting his elder brother Yoritomo, the leader of the Genji, in defeating the Heike. However, defamed by slander and accused by Yoritomo of disloyalty, Yoshitsune was eventually chased away from the capital to the west of Japan.

Two of the incidents that took place on this fugitive journey, as well as the provocative image of the warrior monk Benkei, Yoshitsune's faithful servant, are taken up as the main motifs of this song.

One of the incidents is when Yoshitune has to persuade his lover Shizuka, who is accompanying him on the journey, to return alone to the capital. The scene of Shizuka dancing in tears as she bids farewell to her inurer, resolving to leave him in order to preserve her life for a time when they can meet up again, is the first climax of this song.

The next climax comes with the appearance of the ghost of Tomomori, the Heike General, from the sea. Tomomori, slayed by the Genji in the battle fought on the same sea, tries to revenge himself on Yoshitsune. While Yoshitsune fights the ghost, faithful Benkei, knowing that no ghost is overcome by physical weapons, exorcises the ghost with his prayers. The ghost finally disappears into the sea leaving only white waves, the scene symbolizing peaceful mortality.

All elements are skillfully entwined to set forward the sublime drama: the beauty and faith of Shizuka, the single-hearted loyalty of Benkei, the deep grudge borne by Tomomori's ghost, the momentary spark of life seen in young Yoshitsune, all the more dazzling because of his destiny to perish, and the omnipresent shadow of Yoritomo casting darkness on everyone. Yet all these elements inevitably disappear into the emptiness symbolized by white horses.

Benkei on Board

(Recitation)
The die is cast.
It's time to put on travel gear.
God knows when we shall return!

(Benkei)
I am Benkei,
A monk who lives by the west gate.
Aie. It hurts me even to say this:
My splendid lord, Yoshitsune,
Who should have been at one with his brother,
Yoritomo as sun and moon,
Especially after his dazzling services
In toppling the Heike, their common foe,
Has fallen deep into disgrace instead
Ensnared by wicked slander.
What a fall from power and grace!

In spite of everything,
My lord humbly kept faith
With his brother and has decided to leave the capital
Heading for the West country,

In hopes of gaining time

To convince Yoritomo of his innocence.
Our boat is now making waves
Down the river Yodo
For Daimotsu Bay near Amagasaki.

(Song)
It was the late Twelfth Century.
The sad rift between the ruler,
  The elder brother Yoritomo,
And his brilliant junior,
  Yoshitsune was irremediable.
Yoshitsune's warranted ambitions were crushed.
He had no choice but to abandon the capital
For exile fleeing to the distant West.
The moon seemed never to come out
  From behind the clouds.
He bade farewell to all his memories of the capital.

What a contrast with the last time that he left!
Only a short year ago, he rode out with his troops,
Cheered to the echo by the crowds,
To beat the great Heike rivals for supreme power.
Now his escort were a dozen loyal retainers
Whose shoulders drooped in dejection.

Though the bonding of comrades aboard was close

Their future was as uncertain as that of monks.
No one said a word but everyone knew
Whose cause was just in the eyes of God.
Benkei prayed for his grace
  With his total intensity.

As the boat sailed on, and the waves and tide subsided
Little by little the mood on board relaxed.
By and by they swing into a big bay.

(Benkei)

"If I may be allowed to say so, my Lord,

The presence on this journey of the Lady Shizuka

Might seem ill-advised.

I would suggest, if I may, that at this point

She should return to the capital."

(Yoshitsune)

"Benkei, yes, see that it be done."

(Benkei)

"Certainly, my Lord.

Lady Shizuka. I fear that words may fail me

When I think of the pain you will have to feel,

But I have to convey the reluctant wishes of my Lord

That it would be wise to head back to the capital

Since the mutterings among the men are far from friendly."
The Lady Shizuka, under the threat of separation
At a loss and inconsolable
Burst into tears of utter despair.

Yoshitsune, deeply touched, spoke to her gently:
"It was a totally unexpected misfortune
That made me so suddenly leave the capital.
I deeply appreciate your caring Shizuka
Enough to accompany me on my dangerous way.
But believe me it will be still more hazardous
To sail on against the harsh waves ahead.
It would be better for the future to return to the capital
And bide your time till our return."

Benkei joined Yoshitsune
In giving words of comfort:
"My Lord is simply concerned with the warriors' mood
And you need have no fear at all
That his deep affection for you will ever change."

The Lady Shizuka raised her voice:
"I am a woman of low birth
And so I have no bitter words against my Lord
But please understand that my only wish
Is to pray for a safe and peaceful journey

154

Without rough winds and waves on this fateful trip.
Or do you rather mean to cut short my presence
And so purge the venture of all defilement?"
She shed fierce tears and ingenuously pled
That their love knot should remain tied for ever.
The wind, in its indifference, blew against her.
All of a sudden it dawned on Shizuka
That it was important above all to preserve her life
If she were ever to see her Lord again!

(Yoshitsune)
Benkei, serve *sake* to Shizuka.

(Benkei)
Certainly, my Lord.

(Yoshitune)
"Let us sing a song worthy of your departure.
You can dance with my hat on."
Shizuka stood up and said
"I am hesitant of showing the dance
With my sleeves whirling, though."

(Shizuka's Dance)
An ancient Chinese fable tells of Toh Shukou,
Counselor to Kou-sen, King of Yue,

Who secluded himself in the mountain
To plot a revenge strategy for his King.
Having succeeded in this service,
Toh Shukou saw he should retire,
For Heaven had revealed the Way,
And enjoyed the rest of his life
Boating on the lake.

(Shizuka's Farewell)

"The story has a message to our own selves ……

It is a great sadness for us all

To be leaving the capital behind

And heading for the West against rough seas

With only the pale dawn moon to see us off.

But our humble plea of innocence

Will touch the heart of Yoritomo eventually

If we lie low and behave faithfully.

After all, fraternal ties should never part

Any more than green leaves on a single bough."

(Chorus)

Let us place our trust in the mercy of Yoritomo!

Let us only trust, as our lives accumulate the years

Like wild grasses growing ever thicker!

(Benkei)

Yes, the legend will fulfill its promise

My Lord will once again become a hero!

Let us now embark!

Weigh anchor, sailors, cast away!

(Narration)

Yoshitsune stood out on the deck.

The Lady Shizuka in floods of tears

Took off her hat and mantle in farewell,

A study in lamentation.

Then a turmoil of people arose around the vessel.

Sailors began to shout "Ei-yah, ei-yah"

And finally the boat put out to sea.

(Benkei's Monologue)

By all the Gods!

The wind has turned unexpectedly.

Is this a rush of air from Muko Mountain?

Or from the peaks of Yuzuriha range?

The boat will never arrive at the coast then ……

(Benkei)

Listen, all of the crew,

Pray for God's mercy from the heart!

(Sailors)

Hey, this boat seems haunted by a resentful ghost!

(Benkei)

Oh no. Wait! Never utter

Such an impious thought aboard!

Look, what an eerie scene it is!

The ghosts of all the slaughtered Heike warriors

Are showing their faces

Floating on the waves.

Are they avenging themselves in this timing?

(Yoshitsune)

Where is Benkei?

(Benkei)

Here my Lord.

(Yoshitsune)

You must not let yourself be overawed.

Stay calm.

The Heike have no reason to seek vengeance.

It was their own fault they destroyed themselves.

They defied the benevolence of the Gods and Buddha

And set their faces against divine grace.

That's why they had to suffer punishment and go under.

(Benkei)

All the court nobles of the past Heike regime

Are floating on the waves in a swarm!

(Ghost of Tomomori, Heike's General)

"Let it be known this is the ghost of Tomomori of Heike

Descended in the ninth generation

From the Emperor Kanmu.

Yoshitsune, this really is an unexpected encounter.

The clamour of voices has drawn me and here I find
  your boat.

In just the same way as I was destroyed and went under

You too shall meet your end."

(Chorus)

The ghost picked up a halberd floating on the wave

And grasped also his long crested sward

Passed down from his imperial ancestor.

As he brandished them wildly

And fired off a poisonous breath

Raising up fierce white horses,

The crew became dazzled, disoriented and almost fainted.

Yoshitsune alone did not panic, calmly drew his sword,
And struck the ghost as if he had been a man.

Benkei, knowing no ghost was ever felled by a sword,
Interpolated himself, drew Yoshitsune back,
Began to recite a sutra,
Rubbing his rosary fiercely between his palms
And prayed to the powerful protectors,
The five Myo-ohs, in all the cardinal directions,
East West South North and Centre
To exorcise the ghost.

Benkei's prayer must have reached the Buddha
Because the ghost gradually receded.
Benkei shouted to the sailors to row fast
Leave the area behind and make quickly for the coast.
The ghost fighting to keep in touch
Was warded off by Benkei's prayers and driven out
Fading reluctantly into the distance
Well away from shore.
Look!
Heike's ghosts have disappeared without a trace
White horses' all that's left of them.

Lions—*Father and Son*
(Ren Jishi)
連獅子
Lyrics by Mokuami Kawatake
Music by Shojiro Kineya III

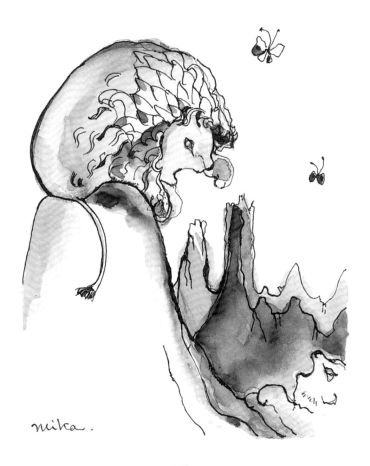

This Nagauta is said to have originated from Noh. A father lion repeatedly strikes his young cub down a cliff towards a deep valley to test his strength and courage. The father lion, greatly satisfied to see his cub's resilience in climbing back time after time, starts dancing in rapture, frolicking about the full blooming peony flowers together with his cub.

It is said that the mythical stone bridge overhanging a deep valley, a ubiquitous symbol in Noh performances, is able to be crossed only by those who have mastered the secret of religious austerities and have achieved a high level of spiritual purity. The lions are the guardians of this bridge, and therefore have to be both strong and noble. The lesson in the song is that ascetic nobility and strength—these concepts that seem to have disappeared from our modern world — are fostered through the bearing of hardships from young age, seen here in the father's rough testing of his son. These lost virtues are still alive in Japanese classical literature, and are a kind of spiritual landscape in the world of Nagauta.

One of the most magnificent dances to be performed on the stage of Kabuki is the scene where the gorgeous lions start to play with tiny butterflies flitting around fragrant peonies in full bloom. Here, the audience is presented with another aesthetic world, watching the lion dancers dancing as if intoxicated, swinging their brightly colored long hair back and forth.

There are two versions of 'Ren Jishi' in Nagauta; one written by Katsusaburo Kineya in 1861, and the revised version written later in 1872 by Shojiro Kineya. The translated version is the latter.

Lions—*Father and Son*

If in the great chain of being
The peony is the king of flowers
The lion is sovereign of animals.

Aureoled like the peonies that are now in full bloom
Outvying the peaches and plums,
Lion the father and his son,
The radiance of whose power
Puts leopards and tigers in the shade,
Are frisking around the foot of the sacred Stone Bridge
To the holy land of contemplation
That is so difficult of access.

As everyone knows, the bridge
Is overhung high in the sky
By the Seiryo mountain
Where the Bodhisattva of wisdom is said to dwell.
Looking up you will see a waterfall pouring down
An immeasurable cliff-face through the clouds.

Looking down you will hear
The winds blow and their furious echoes
Bellow through an abyss of pines.

Behold the legendary bridge!
It reaches out as a huge rainbow emerging after rain
To reflect the glow of sunset.

Father lion came up to his son,
  suddenly he turfed the youngster
From the top of the peak into the bottom of the valley,
As if testing his son's resilience!
The poor lion cub tumbled down
Rolling over and over down and down.
Into the depth of the valley.
He then firmly picked himself up again
And scrambled back to the top with his tiny claws.

The father knocked his son off again
And again,
Again and again the son climbed back.

Little by little the father's rough demeanor softened
As he saw his son was fully worthy
To guard the approaches of the bridge
And now his eyes were caught
By the tiny sunlit sails of butterflies
As they flitted round the peonies.
They floated in and out of flower shades
And hid beneath the leaves

Lions—*Father and Son*

Like acrobatic spirits in the breeze
Playing hide-and-seek with the lions.

Both butterflies and lions seemed a little intoxicated
Tacking crazily around each other.

Then a sonorous tune of flutes and *koto* began to sound
And a ballet of delicate sleeves and dancers
Rotated in the sky.

The fragrance of the peonies soaked the air
And two lions like a human pair
With lion heads on their shoulders
Broke into an enraptured dance to a joyful counterpoint
  of hand drums and shouting.

Crowned with tassels of gold,
Inspired divinely, they leapt
Among the peonies and boughs.
All the plants prostrated themselves
Before this ecstatic energy.

Blessed by the immortal power
Father lion and son alike in perfect poise and dignity
Assumed the rightful throne
Of an invocation rightly celebrated.

Dojo Temple of Kishu
(Kishu Dojo Ji)
紀州道成寺
Lyrics based on a Noh song
Music by Saburosuke Kineya V

Dojo Temple of Kishu

The origin of the legend of Dojo Ji is said to date back to the Heian era (8th to 12th century). The legend was used first as the theme of a Noh play, and then converted to a Kabuki dance in the Edo era. The story is thrilling and full of highlight scenes. A young handsome monk 'Anchin' and beautiful young girl 'Kiyo-Hime' fall in love, but the monk chooses to abandon her to pursue his strict Buddhist discipline. The girl transforms herself into a serpent to take revenge upon him and follows him all the way to Dojo Ji.

There are many variations to this song and dance performance, but the most wellknown among Kabuki performances is called 'Kyo-Ganoko Musume Dojo Ji,' which is often used as a test piece to evaluate the dancing skill of Kabuki actors. The one closest to the original Noh song is 'Kishu Dojo Ji.'

Dojo Ji station is on the Kisei line of Japan Railway, not far from Wakayama city, the capital of Wakayama Prefecture situated in Ki-i peninsula in the west of Japan. The famous temple is only fifteen minutes away from the station on foot. The atmosphere of the place is relaxed and pleasant, with an old belfry standing quietly in the ground. When I visited the temple with a friend, I noticed there was no bell in the bell tower and pointed this out to my friend, who laughed at my ignorance and reminded me that this was because the bell had been melted by the fire of Kiyo-Hime's jealousy.

Since the old days, female obsession is said to be something to beware of. There is the story of Salome who asks Herod for the head of John the Baptist as a reward for her dancing. It is all the more terrifying to know the context for this wish, which was that she was competing against her own mother for his love. Compared to Salome's, Kiyo-Hime's obsession was not so gruesome. What happened to Anchin, who was hiding inside the bell? Was he burnt to ashes or did he manage to escape? In the Nagauta it is only said that he had "gone and disappeared," without any indication of whether he escaped safely or not. Perhaps this song also illustrates the female view of the sex-wars: that men are pleased with fulfilling their selfish desires alone... it is as if we can hear such a line coming always from the chorus.

167

Dojo Temple of Kishu

The Dojo Temple was named in memory of its founder
Ki-no-Michinari, or Dojo.
Pilgrims follow the road signs
To the entrance gate of Buddha's world
Where voices in the tranquil air
Calmly recite the sutras
That extend a golden gleam to bridge
Buddha's hand and our own world
And save so many from its suffering.
If you cleave to the laws of the sutra,
Buddha will mercifully erase your faults
Of self interested and unfair pleas,
Of vows subscribed on a whim and
Of wrong-doings fuelled by desire.

Waves of people are trooping by
To hold a memorial service
In the shadow of the temple bell.
As the pale moon is setting high tide is on its way.
Mist covers the pine beech,
The remains of the day still linger in the sky.
The pilgrims are happy to arrive
In time to view the sunset.

Noble men wearing high hats

Seem to set the rhythm for dance.

Pale snow lingering on my fleeting life
Melted away as spring rain fell.
Here come the flowers and willow buds.
Seasons revolve and so do their tune
But my delusive desires never melt.
The moon always shines aloof in the serene sky
But this lower world is full
Of ever-changing messy frictions.
A Chinese youth of old Kantan thought he had dreamed
A very long lift-history in his nap.
But he realized when he woke up
The nap had been all too short.
The ebb and flow of life are
As evanescent as a blinking of the eye.

Let's decorate each crown with flowers,
Spread out our sleeves like peacocks
And join the parade of festive people milling round.
Everyone is dancing! What a joy!

Cherry blossoms in a frame of pine green....
Temple bells ringing
To the background of the sunset....

When I came to the temple on the mount

Cherry blossoms fell to the rhythm of the evening bell;
The winds sounded from the four corners of the campus.
I knew as the moon set and the birds sang
That frosts were about to bind the earth;
The tide was ebbing, the fishermen's lights floated away;
And so did peoples' distress and the grief of the day
As they settled down to sleep in a night of peace.

Who is the rascal there trying to sneak up to the bell
Counting the time of darkness and to ring the hours?
His mind is changed with the very thought
Of the dark hatred of a woman that haunts the bell.
He ran into the house nearby
With his cloth hung over his head
Immediately after having touched
  the cannon instead.

If you listen to the history of the temple,
You will have tears of sorrow for a monk
Who broke the strict rule that prohibits
  the presence of women.

Long ago a villager called Shoji
Had a pretty daughter whom he dearly loved.
Every year a young priest, a mountain guide of Kumano,
  visited him and stayed with them.
Before anyone knew, the young priest and the daughter

Dojo Temple of Kishu

Frequently shared a pillow of grass
Under the concealing fog.
The young woman did not care her ears
Should be drenched with nasty dews
But cling with delight to the handsome priest
And vowed never be apart from him in life.
It's hard not to be moved by her desperate plight.

The priest faced a dilemma;
If he went astray and chose their path of earthy love,
He had to abandon the Buddhist discipline
And nullify all the efforts he had made for years.
His one escape was to run out of the house
Like an arrow cutting through the dark sky
And to disappear, he hoped, into thin air.

The daughter, having detected her lover's flight
Chased him in desperation
But the river was swollen with bad luck
And she realized there was no way to cross.
But what alternative could there be?
So she jumped into the raging river
Amidst the whirling white horses
Driven by a woman's uncontrollable urge.
Poor woman! Her body hardly floated
And little by little turned into a snake
Who swam the river to reach the temple

171

But was unable to find a place to hide.

The serpent found the bell pulled down,
Held the metal holder in her mouth and
Twined her body round its huge circumference.
Look! The bell was wholly melted
By the fire of her flaring grudge.

The priest had gone and disappeared.

It is terrifying to think
That her jealousy still haunts the spot
And casts an evil spell over innocent visitors.

Villagers prayed and recited ardently
A sutra for the permanent protection of Buddha
And its power incorporated in the creed
Even if all the sands on the river bed
Turned to cinders in the flame of her jealousy.

Oh the five Great Myo-ohs sitting at the four corners
And the centre of the universe!
We believe you grant us great wisdom when we listen
And you guide us to your own Pure Land.
By taming our wild desires
Once we know ourselves with humility....

Responding to the prayer,
The bell appeared again in its original shape
And began to ring with no one striking it.
Behold! a serpent woman came out of it
Draped at the top of the bell tower.

Dragon Kings of East, West and the Centre of the Universe!
And other Dragon Kings of the Indian world!
We pray for the acceptance of our plea
And for protection against any evil spell!

Surely the prayer should be undermining her grudge;
The serpent suddenly jumped up and lay flat
Repeatedly in her acute anguish
While she threw burning breath at the bell
Which burned herself as well.
In the end the serpent had to throw herself.
Into the river Hidaka.

Priests, who were praying hard, saw
The sutra had finally ultimate power
To lay the evil spirit of the serpent
And returned, satisfied but abstracted,
To their lodging in the courtyard.

Girls in Blossom Season
—*Wasting Time on Their Way Home*
(Tenarai-Ko)
手習い子
Lyrics by Kinpachi Masuyama
Music by Shojiro Kineya I

Girls in Blossom Season—*Wasting Time on Their Way Home*

This song is said to have been composed in 1789 for a Kabuki dance performance, almost 100 years before the Meiji Restoration. Young girls on the brink of maturity are wasting time in the spring breeze on the way home from lessons. Are the young girls today the same? Unlike those in this Nagauta, aren't the girls who attend cram schools today coming home with exhausted hollow expressions? Some may say "Not to worry. They are much tougher than you would think." I certainly hope they are.

Spring sunshine makes us feel happy. The song depicts carefree girls strolling back from lessons, recollecting their teacher's reproaches or praises. The teacher's advice about love and jealousy —— "The taste of first love is like a real jewel; it should not be spoiled by careless jealousy, for jealousy makes horns grow out of one's forehead!" —— is, as yet, too abstract for them to comprehend. However, feeling a bit matured and proud to have been given such advice, they are going home at leisure, wasting time on their ways, taking surreptitious glances at each other to judge signs of friends' physical maturity.

Such a laid-back peaceful world of youth as represented in this Nagauta seems to have been lost from our modern Japanese society. This type of scene is not even depicted in comic books anymore. Japanese youth have developed a tolerance for the most overbearing imagery, and have lost all sensitivity towards appreciating the inner landscape. Outside of Japan I have found that sensitivity towards the simple pleasures of life is still alive, passed preciously from parent to child.

It seems to me that Tenarai-Ko is a sharp warning to our contemporary society in this sense, and would like to ask my readers if they share this opinion.

175

Girls in Blossom Season
—Wasting Time on Their Way Home

Yoshino mountains are decorated

With full bloom of cherry blossoms.

And adorable young girls are seen

Under the shade of flowers

Attracting endless strollers.

A little too young are the girls

Like small buds of late coming cherries.

But unexpectedly people encounter

One of the girls with a mature appeal

Who is on her way home from a lesson

  off the route though.

Is her coquettish hairdo with little flowers

A hint of a secret love?

Look! Isn't she a flirt with kimono frivolously swaying?

Another girl playing with paper string for fortunetelling

Wears an affected obi of pretty satin

And her long sleeves are printed with plum flower patterns.

Her obi is loosening though but her smile is so lovely.

"The taste of first love is a real jewel;

It should not be spoiled by a careless jealousy

For it may produce an ugly horn on your face".

That's what your teacher said. How awful!

I will certainly take her advice.

But who knows! She is still too young

And too innocent to overview the future.

You guys shouldn't look down on these girls

Even if they look like flappers.

They are diligently taking hard lessons

Of traditional *koto*, *shamisen* and dancing.

They know how to behave themselves

But are mute on ardent emotions

Hidden within hearth of their hearts.

For they may have headaches

With capricious boy friends.

So girls may surely have grudges against them.

Nasty boys must once have given them sweet excitement

When their black hair were totally tangled

But now they must have flung them away!

Boys are surely wicked!

Girls are also sinful being easily allured

By sweet but empty flattery,

"Pretty as a cherry flower!"

And they abandon boy friends one by one.
Girls are equally wreck,
East country girls in particular!

Even a quiet love when it gets harder
Suddenly splashes out unfriendly rumour.
The moment of lovers' satisfaction
And proud fulfillment never stay long.
For it is the law of uncertainty.

Nevertheless men are always mad about love;
Any time when they feel it's sweet smell,
Suddenly they get absent-minded,
Become sober and forget about drinking.
They would even gear up
To climb across the high mountains
To the final destination, Kyoto,
The terminal of the road to lust!

The young lady is praying,
'Please, my protector, God Sugawara,
Make my man stop his love hunting.
As I promise, I will surely get rid
Even of my favorite plum fruits
For my entire life for his *sake*.'

Girls in Blossom Season—*Wasting Time on Their Way Home*

Her praying posture is so elegant and innocently sincere.

Young girls talk and talk merrily

Like spring birds chirping.

Their lovely voices dance in the wind

As if stretching wings from bough to bough.

Those dolls are pretty petals

  of plums and camellias

To snow the flowery chapeau

And to deepen the beauty

  of the spring scene.

A Circuitous Path to Revenge
—*The Story of Kuranosuke Oishi*
(Uki Daijin)

有喜大尽―大石内蔵助物語―

Lyrics by Choji Nakauchi
Music by Jokan Kineya and Kosaburo Yoshizumi Ⅳ

A Circuitous Path to Revenge—*The Story of Kuranosuke Oishi*

'Chushin-Gura' is still one of the most entertaining and widely-loved plays among all Kabuki performances. It is a revenge play by the Ako soldiers in honor of the head of their clan, who was ordered to perform 'Seppuku (Harakiri)' by the Tokugawa government. Uki-Daijin was composed in the end of the Meiji era (1909), and is rather factual lyrics depicting not the historically famous revenge story itself, but the portrait of Yoshio Oishi, the leader of the avenging soldiers and the central figure in the story. In a sense, the lyrics are surely the product of the modern Meiji era, which was different from the preceding Edo era with its feudalism and conservatism.

Some intellectuals abroad may regard such old-fashioned revenge for a feudal master as a despicable act. However, in our ancient feudal system, loyalty to one's master was considered to be of absolute and utmost importance, and therefore, any revenge for a master was morally acceptable. Yet, because a murder was not legally permitted, the 47 Ako soldiers who participated in the act of vengeance were ordered to kill themselves by 'Harakiri.'

Although the drama itself is bloody, the lyric is about Oishi playing lavishly and gracefully in the pleasure district of Kyoto to disguise his intentions of revenge. Such a life of pleasure, while it was also a way of camouflage, may also have been his last worldly joy after his decision to submit himself to death. The scene representing his complex emotions - his readiness to give himself up, feeling of regret to leave worldly pleasures, heartfelt loyalty to his master and faith in what he is going to do - is the highlight of the lyrics.

In 'Ichi-Riki,' the famous 'ryoutei' (restaurant) still in business in the Gion district of Kyoto, the posthumous tablets of the 47 Ako soldiers are still enshrined to this day.

A Circuitous Path to Revenge
—*The Story of Kuranosuke Oishi*

(Orgy at The Tea House)
Calm down and rest a while
Or you will find yourself at the heart
Of a nasty scandal spreading far and wide.
Staying up all night isn't a problem.
I can just as well sleep tomorrow.

(Kiken, a visiting Samurai)
"You should know that I am the man of men
Of the whole country of Kyushu
And I have come to meet Oishi.
Please let me in!"

Let's have a flower dance
All together! Dance!

(Kiken)
"The lantern here says 'Sasa-ya'
And I'm sure it's Oishi's favorite haunt
Where he drinks and enjoys himself.
Please let me in!

What a strange place this is!

No one seems to pay the slightest attention

To my request though I'm as polite as I know how.

Have they all lost their heads?

A samurai up from the country, like myself,

Never can understand the rules

Of those red lantern places.

Pardon my manners, but I'm coming in!"

(Narration)

Oishi's nickname, 'Uki' is ambiguous.

Literally, it means 'Having Joy.'

But joy for what? Having affairs? What else?

Oishi stirred up by girls

Was deep in his cups, in a good mood but wild.

Who would imagine his shameful drinking had a purpose?

Oishi prayed his secret would never leak.

Watching a remote grass fire in the mid night

Oishi heaved a deep sigh of sympathy with it.

My fleeting life will soon go up in smoke.

Why not spend the rest of it

In this lavish court of a red lantern?

(Oishi)

"Oh! It's you, sir, Mr. Kiken!

We met yesterday over at Gion.

Welcome, welcome.

Where's the master?

Come out and greet the guest!

This gentleman is a samurai

Who once served the Lord of Satsuma;

The one famous for capturing

That villain Bonji-Kuro not long ago,

You remember, at Suzaku boulevard.

Wouldn't you mind a little tepid *sake*?"

Oishi urged the master;

"Do gather as many girls as you can

And be sure he is served

Without any offhand manners!"

The master understanding what was said

And not said, replied "Yes sir, yes sir"

And turned to his wife:

"You heard all that?"

"Yes, of course. Understood!"

(Chorus)

Colorful fans light up the dance

In the delicate fingers of girls' hands,

Snowflakes whirling in their sleeves.

The sake is shot through with a golden hue

Springing from the bottom of the glass,

An inexhaustible gushing well.
Pleasure spills over as it always does.

(Kiken)

Kiken spoke stiffly, with his knee drawn up,

"My first taste of *sake* in such a lavish place

Is rather disgusting. Or, are you saying, Oishi,

That it actually tastes good?

I hear you indulge every night

In an orgy of drinking and womanizing here.

I can never make out what you are thinking.

What are you really about?",

Kiken pressed on.

(Oishi)

"What? You want to know my story?"

Oishi looked at him, quietly and with suspicion.

(Kiken)

"Tell me what you are keeping to yourself!"

(Oishi)

"This is a great honour!

You are asking me to expose....

My latest lyrics of my song!

I will be delighted to sing it for you

As an appetizer for more drink!"

Oishi took up the shamisen and sang in a drowsy way.

From the bridge of Shijo
The light of lantern is seen.
Only a light is seen.
Is that the light of Tea House 'Niken'?
Is that 'Niken'?
Or that of 'Maruyama'?
Ah yes, it must be 'Maruyama'.

(Kiken)
"Such a lousy song makes me sleepy.
I didn't come here to listen to your song.
Now I know as the rumour says
That you do not have the slightest intention
Of carrying out the revenge."

(Oishi)
"Not the slightest intention!"

(Kiken)
"You really are a disgrace to the name of samurai!
This falling by the wayside is inexcusable.
You are even making a mockery of your own name

Oishi, the 'heavy stone'. You are the lightest of stones

A pumice, low down the chain of being,

Nothing serious!"

(Oishi)

"Ah but my name also means 'Have Joy'".

(Kiken)

"Hold up your tongue, pumice!

Pension parasite!

You are only a dog beneath your samurai skin.

Crawl! I say, crawl here, ignoble dog!"

(Narration)

Oishi, apparently awed by the insults,

Crawled before Kiken;

Who got still more excited and shouted

Pulling up his kimono and showing his hairy knees

"Eat this pickled octopus from the dish on the floor

  like a dog!"

As Oishi was about to put his chin out,

Kiken kicked him with his foot

And vanished like a ghost into the dark.

The dense curtain of night was falling

  on the red lantern courtyard.

All that luxury floated on the glittering lights
Now turned into a dead silence of dreams.
Do storms nowhere hide seed of violence
Which might blow off peaceful flowers?

(Dialogue of Oishi and Ukihashi, his lover)

(Ukihashi)
Even the fresh spring field
Has to reckon with the heartless shower
Damping down the insects chorus.
My deep sorrow goes nowhere
But is holed up in my tiny self.
I know my black hair is disheveled
On my breast. Who cares?
I don't know to whom I can open up.
Though my hair is shown up to advantage
By an exquisite boxwood comb
My nightly duties to serve men
Without even the faintest tie as dew
Are so hard to endure
Tears fall and make my sleeves all wet.

(Oishi)
"It's you, Ukihashi, my love."

(Ukihashi)

"Oh, dearest Uki-sama !* (*Oishi's nick Name)

It is surely a joy to meet you

But your hidden mission casts a pall

On our encounters every time

As salt water might invade a lake.

On whom can I depend in the future?

Am I the same homeless fowl that sleeps every night

While floating on the waves?

I wish I could desolve like a bubble.

Uki-sama, soon I shall leave for long."

(Oishi)

"What do you mean?"

(Ukihashi)

Even if I firmly abandon this life and vanish like a bubble

You will never really feel the loss.

Tomorrow I will leave this court married off in the east,

To pay a debt of my folks

Which is what happens to girls like me.

(Oishi)

"You have decided to start a new life?"

(Ukihashi)

"Good luck in your quest to nail the villain...."

(Oishi)

"Oh no. Please calm down..

My lucky pillow is stained
With sweat and dirt.
My body is getting thinner
And my clothes are frayed:
Where am I heading?

Ukihashi, I need hardly say, you are a wonderful girl
Being the sister of Sampei, my comrade.
If our plan was successfully carried out
Thanks to your faithful help Sampei and your father, too,
Who had spent an unhappy life
Will surely attain an eternal peace
  at the Buddhist's paradise."

Oishi and Ukihashi exchanged cups of *sake*,
Each feeling loath to part from the other.

(Monologue of Ukihashi)
My sleeves can hardly wrap around
And hold dews on flowers

A Circuitous Path to Revenge—The Story of Kuranosuke Oishi

Or the hail dropped on bamboo grass,
So it could be harder still to contain
My tears and stop them overflowing.
I sacrificed myself to help my parents
And all my family
Falling into this miserable life.
But the serene moon must know
The sorrow hidden in my heart.
Wherever I live in the east apart from you,
I wish I shall always meet you
In my dreams and convey
My feelings to you by messenger birds.

Ukihashi in fact kept her word
And devotedly kept tabs on every move
Of the foe for Oishi.

(Coda)
Breaking the silence of the dawn
The signaling drum was struck
To marshal the Ako samurais
For the march to avenge
By their devotion to the death
The injustice done to their Lord
Forced to commit hara-kiri in despair.

Dirty Spider
(Tsuchi Gumo)
土蜘

Lyrics based on Tokiwazu
Music by Kangoro Kineya III

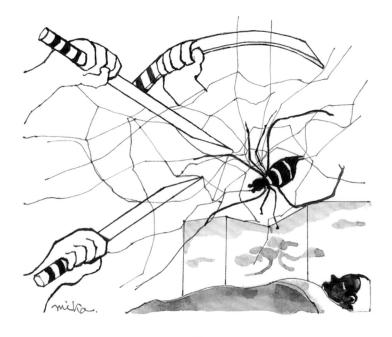

Great scholars in the field of Nagauta such as the late Dr. Gyokuto Asakawa and Dr. Koichi Ikeda have accomplished deep and thorough research regarding the legend of Dirty Spider (the Earth Spider) and its historical background in classical art. Therefore, I will refer those who are interested in these topics to their works, and would like to touch upon the charm of this Nagauta.

Unlike some Nagauta composed for Kabuki dance performances, this Nagauta was composed as a song to be sung on its own in 1862, based on a Tokiwazu song called 'Kumo no Ito (Spider Gossamer).'

Both originate from the same legend: a hideous spider monster disguised as a lovely little girl tries to attack the famous General Yorimitsu who is ill in his bed.

An earth spider is very small, and makes its pouch-like nest under the ground. It is actually not that threatening of a spider. Some of the readers may recall digging out their nests to capture them in childhood. However, some spiders are said to he poisonous enough to affect human brain functions. Once I was in a taxi up in a mountain in Izu Peninsula and told a driver that I found, a large spider on my head in Izu. The driver then replied, "Oh, I know. It's the one like a tarantula." Not expecting to hear such a foreign word coming out of somebody who looked rather like a country bumpkin, I was surprised, as well as frightened to know that such dangerous creatures exist in the area I live.

The Spider in this lyric is in fact a monster, and symbolizes the popular resistance against the hegemonic power represented by Yorimitsu. On a dark stormy flight, when warriors on duty are tense and expecting something to happen, a tiny doll-like maid appears. A conversation takes place between a warrior and this girl, which gradually builds up further tension until the climax. Just as the disguise is revealed, the girl-turned-spider tries to dash into Yorimitsu's bedroom. The structure of the story is based on the classic pattern seen in Noh performances called "Jo-Ha-Kyu" (introduction-explosion-rapid finale).

Most monsters appearing in Japanese classic art disappear into the void, rather than killed bleeding or injured. I wonder if this is because of the tender national character of us Japanese, or if it is for the *sake* of the audience so that they can go home in peace.

Dirty Spider

Behold the clouds!
Endlessly they emerge and disappear,
As if they are in thrall to the will of the winds.

(Monologue of General Yorimitsu)
"I have to be aware of my life
Exactly like the foam of water streams
Unsettled as they gush and vanish!"

The illness of General Yorimitsu is very serious
And his mental pain is even greater,
For with him there is no question of sparing
Anyone else or indeed himself.
Night-shift warriors on duty
Heavily guarded his residence
Encased in elaborate security precautions.

All kinds of medicine and exorcism
Were tried but failed to work.
Yorimitsu, such a great general
Of whom even ogres might be frightened,
Was now totally distressed,
Full of remorse at his own lack of precautions,
And gasping for breath as he lay.
The night was blowing a furious gale.

The warriors on duty warming themselves up
Puffing heavily on their pipe tobacco.
Smoke rose from the ashtrays.
It was two o'clock in the dead of night.
The darkness was steadily growing deeper.

All of a sudden, a tiny maid appeared;
A lovely doll probably raised in the city.
Showing her back view
She toddled along with a thread
Hanging from her hair neatly cut and bundled,
And handed out tea for warriors.
When she was propositioned she winked back
Her eyes narrowed charmingly
But she shook her head and refused to be tempted.

"You should pick before the rain starts"
Is a rule in harvesting tea leaves
As the trees grow fast on the hilly plantations,
But mind the rule is only for tea not girls.

The maid, in a very frolicsome mood,
Distributed tea to them, one by one.

(Warrior)
"What a lovely girl! ventured a warrior.
Whose daughter are you?"

(Maid, in fact a spider or evil spirit)
"I am a frail creature like a translucent spider web
Hanging from the ruined eaves.
But so what?"

(Warrior)
"How old are you?"

(Spider)
"How old am I?"

(Warrior, singing)
How old are you, my dear Moon?

(Spider, also in singing)
Thirteen and seven years old.

(Warrior)
"What if the moon is clouded?"

(Spider)
"Why not let me blow off the nasty clouds?"

(Warrior)
"How do you see the boundless universe
Once the clouds have been cleared?"

(Spider)

"It is my high ambition to rise endlessly into the lucid sky
Like a kite with the thread
Stretched as long as your imagination."

(Warrior)

"What if the thread is cut and you fall down?"

(Spider)

"I just revert to the ground."

(Warrior)

"What is the origin of 'Hide and seek'?"

(Spider)

"The Goddess Amaterasu hid herself
In the giant rock. That was the folk tale
And now the children are still playing that game."

(Warrior)

"What is your view of the Doll's Festival?"

(Spider)

"It's a charming rehearsal for a wedding banquet."

(Warrior)

"For Boy's Festival people decorate
Carp-shaped streamers and war helmets.
How do you interpret the boys playing
With threads woven from iris leaves
And with delicate swords?"

(Spider)
"It's embryonic martial arts.
Let me hold the rein like this
And put my feet on those shells.
I will march as if riding a real horse.
Look at this!
Jingle-jangle! Jingle-jangle!
Ride the horse firmly and hold the rein tight
With the bit raised high."

(Warrior)
"Are you riding OK?"

(Spider)
"I'm riding alright!"

(Warrior)
"Hold on! Something strange is happening!
The winds are behaving weirdly!"

While murmuring

"Let me go, let me go,"
The Spider quickly revealed its real identity as a monster
And tried to rush into the bedroom of General Yorimitsu.

"This is an outrage!"
The warriors all pulled up their sleeves
And tried to block the sudden invasion.
But the spider was shrewdly evading
The warriors' defense,
  emerging here and vanishing there.
He enjoyed perfect command
Of his supernatural powers.

"What a treacherous rascal you are!"
As they waved their swords around.
But he always escaped their efforts,
Dauntless and unscathed.

Just as the moon at dawn
Is easily missed when you try to trace him,
He moved so nimbly
That no one could begin to catch him
And finally they failed to capture
The villain spider, the dirty monster.

Devil Fox in China
(Sangoku Youko Monogatari)
三国妖狐物語
Lyrics by an anonymous writer
Music by Rokushiro Kineya I

A fox disguised as a beautiful princess often appears in old legends, as in the case of this Nagauta. According to this long song, composed of three volumes, the mischievous fox spirit had the final goal of transforming India, the birthplace of holy Buddha, into a world of demons. However, failing to do this in India, the fox tried to do the same in China, failed again, and finally came to Japan (Nasu Moor in Tochigi Prefecture), where his attempt failed yet again. The ending, though, is a happy one: the fox reformed itself and was finally reincarnated as a god.

This grand fiction, involving the three different countries as its background, was first used for a Kabuki performance in the mid 19th century. Its origin is said to be found in a Noh song called 'Sessho-Seki,' literally translated as 'killing stones.' 'Sessho seki' stones, found in the mountainside of Nasu, are in fact volcanic lavas, and were given such a name because the sulfuric gas hanging in the air often killed animals coming near the stones.

The 'fox of golden fur with nine tails' escaped India and came to China, disguising itself as the beautiful wife of King Chu of the state of Yin. However, the disguise was revealed by a spy who came to rescue King Bun of the Thou Dynasty, who had been captured by King Chu, and the fox flew away to Japan. The route the fox took from India to China to Japan is the route along which Buddhism spread. I admire the author of this story who thought of using this same route for the devil fox's flight. Whoever it was, the author from the 19th century had a rich imagination comparable to that of a spy novel author in the 21st century. It is also rather amusing when we think of the ending, when the fierce fox, after its long and dynamic flight across vast countries, loses its power in Japan — its last station — and is finally tamed.

Devil Fox in China

The captured King Bun of the state of Zhou
Woke up and looked around:
'Ah, it was a dream.

I saw clearly the Dandoku Mountain in India.
Ricksha and stablemen were talking
  about the treacherous creatures
Once rampant there in millions
  during the past centuries
But now flown away to China.
I look around and realize
This is a gorgeous Chinese Palace!'

'I saw my lovely son, Kinsha,
In the middle of a huge court-yard
Tightly strapped by an iron chain.
My wife, having fainted,
Had wholly lost her sight. What a misery!'

Even the sun and the moon are forced to vanish
  by the storm;
So is human life obstructed and removed
By truly unexpected disasters.

King Bun was resigned to his fate
And listened quietly to music played on *koto*.

When the night's sky is clear
I can see the plum flower clearly.
In this sheer darkness, however,
Groping is my only way to reach you.
Our encounter should be concealed
 from prying eyes.
But your enchanting perfume
Transferred to my sleeves cannot be concealed
Revealing our secret love.

When the golden brocade was rolled up
King Chu of the state of Yin was seen
Sitting on the gorgeous throne;
'Ha, ha. Your voice is so sweet
Unchanged ever since those days
Beautifully matched with Japanese *koto*.'
He praised his wife, Dakki, and held her closer.
Leaning upon her, he looked
 like an ugly and devilish flower.
Dakki responded to him with a demure smile
Like a small tiger lily;
Her flirting eyes were saying 'Don't desert me ever!'

(King Chu)

"The prisoners captured of late have been mere farmers.

There's no glory in that for me.

The one that matters today is King Bun

Who ruled a significant state.

I will get his son's belly chopped up

  and will have a drink while tasting

His parents' screaming as a relish."

He ordered an executioner to prepare.

The executioner divined what was wanted

  and stood up.

The mother of the son, Kinsha, woke up

Then, screaming madly in anguish.

But just as she was about to run to the child

The executioner killed her with a single thrust

And said to Dakki

"Please sing one more song for the king

While I cook up the dish."

I wonder if the shower has started?

Listening through the thin wooden door

I feel my love taking ever deeper root

As I share a pillow with you.

The man named as the executioner
In fact simply pretended to cut up
The son's belly and to put it on the plate.
He almost spoke aloud "Here you are,
My King!"
When he judged it exactly the right moment.
He extracted from his costume
A special mirror for eradicating devils.

What an incredible miracle!
Dakki suddenly started to thrash around.
King Bun now shed the iron chain
And pointed the mirror to her.
Instantly Dakki stood revealed as a devil
A fox of golden hair with nine tails.

(King Chu)
"Good Heavens! My Empress was a devil!
However, even if you were a devil
You are the partner of my sleep."

(Devil Fox)
"You are such a treacherous fool
Bad king of silliness and low talent;

Inferior even to all animals,

You shall be overthrown here today;

In fact, the time of a new state, Shu,

  may have come.

This is what my intuition had foreseen

Rooted in my stupid wish.

But I was trapped alas by a dirty trick

Of the spies of King Bun.

Now my real figure has been revealed,

And my wish has been disregarded.

Why not migrate to the East? — Japan!"

The devil fox vanished on these words

And disappeared into the vacant sky.

The Fisherman and Woodcutter
(Gyoshou Mondou)
漁樵問答
Lyrics by an anonymous writer
Music by Shojiro Kineya III

The Fisherman and Woodcutter

This Nagauta is the combination of two famous children's stories 'Urashima Taro' ('Taro of Urashima') and 'Yourou no Taki' ('Healing Water Fall for the Aged'), and can be considered a fun and lighthearted story. It was composed in 1879 (10th year of Meiji) and is regarded as a suitable piece for a dance performance because of its clear plot.

The story is quite simple. An old woodcutter found a water fall in the mountains and was surprised to find out that the water had magical healing powers. He came across Urashima Taro, who had just been back from the Sea God's Palace, and they started a merry conversation boasting the merits of the mountain and the sea, and drinking the holy water which turns into '*sake*' as they drink. As they happily got drunk, Urashima Taro opened a magic casket of souvenirs from the sea, which was forbidden to be opened. As a result, he turned into an old man, while the woodcutter became a young man with black hair. The repenting Urashima and the joyful woodcutter both went down the mountain, celebrating long and happy living.

The story is quite ironic. Maybe the god turned Urashima into an old man because he had experienced enough joy from indulging in the love affair with the sea goddess, and likewise turned the diligent old woodcutter into a young man so that he could restart enjoying his life, taking pity that his entire life had been devoted to work.

Even water turns into '*sake*' to give us miracle power and energy, depending on the spirit ('ki'—— mental energy) of its drinker. This is also a lesson suggested in this simple yet pleasant story.

The Fisherman and Woodcutter

The waterfall sunk in the mountains is coming into sight
And mirrors the glitter of countless splashes of green pines.

The old man climbs up the familiar track
Though it is getting harder at his age
Bearing brushwood on his shoulders.
Totters up and struggles to the grass
Near the basin of the fall to take a rest.

As he looks up at the sky the mountains loom so high.
The fall roars as it plunges down
Leaps and spumes and splashes fiercely.
The wild streams tumbling through
The rocks strewn in the river are
Assumed to be sacred as a water
That heals the aged of their aches.

Yes, it is healing water for the aged;
Its roaring sound and holy nature
Have reached the Emperor's ear.
What greater honour could they be!
The woodcutter prays that the fall
Should not conceivably run dry

And, leaves the site warm with his belief.

Then there appears Taro Urashima
A fisherman who has just been back
From the Sea God's Palace
Carrying a heavy casket of souvenir.
It seemed quite useless and simply heavy
And a nuisance, though he has been asked
Never to open it except in an emergency.
The casket is a kind of penalty
For his voluptuous love affairs
With the reigning beauties of the palace.
Grumbling at the burden he has to bear
He trudges by with his fishing tackle on his back.

For one to whom travel has so far been
On a turtle's back in the sea
Deep mountain paths are fresh and strange.
Here is an unwonted encounter
Between a fisherman and a woodcutter.
They sit together in cordial greeting.
"Whom do I have the pleasure of talking to?"
Urashima asks.
"I am a woodcutter living hereabouts,"
He replies and adds

"How come, you, a most unexpected visitor,

Should turn up in this place?"

"I have returned from the Sea God's palace

At the far end of the waves of the sea"

Urashima replies.

Oh, yes? Yes!

Their conversations get under way.

At sea, you have whale and shark fishing......

In the mountains, tiger and wolf hunting, too......

The sound of the wave is like the rhythm of drums......

The sound of the wind is like a melody......

Washing feet in the blue sea-water......

Washing ears by the serene fountain......

The superb taste of baby fishes held by ospreys......

The superb taste of *sake* brewed by monkeys......

But the water scooped from this waterfall

Has a taste of mountain sage

Containing a magic that turns it into *sake*

Which should heal the aged as the legend says.

Let's take the water!

Urashima looked at his casket and murmurs

"It was given me to open only in an emergency to be tackled

urgently……"

What should I do?

While gulping up *sake* in his hands he makes up his mind

And opens the casket.

All of a sudden, white smoke shoots up

And that splendidly young man, Urashima,

Turns promtly into an old man with frosty hair

  and the old woodcutter

Becomes a young man with a very handsome head of black

  hair indeed.

They looked one another in the face.

Urashima repents hard of his haste

And the woodcutter drinks with joy

Of the sacred *sake*.

While saddled with their changed situations

They are now, each of them, walking home.

They are celebrating together,

A happy path toward a long and happy rest of life.

A Scouring Rush Picker
(Tokusa Gari)
木賊刈り

Lyrics originated from a Noh song
Music by Shojiro Kineya I

This Nagauta was composed in 1798 based on the Noh song 'Tokusa.' A young boy named Matsuwaka who is looking for his lost father comes to the Sonohara Mountain in Shinano (presently Nagano Prefecture) accompanied by a monk, and encounters his father who was picking rushes there. However, the Nagauta has no relation to this original story, and instead only describes the sentiment of a solitary rush picker working in the mountains.

Although solitary, the rush picker is not at all feeling lonely. Positively taking pleasure in improving his old age, he shares with the moon that shines in the sky the memory of a famous old anecdote: "Once upon a time, there lived a grandpa and a grandma. Every morning grandpa went up into the mountain to collect firewood, and grandma went down the river to wash their clothes." The old man walks along a mountain path, smiling to himself as he recites this familiar anecdote which we, including myself, all heard repeatedly when young. He then thinks of his old wife waiting for him, probably feeling the harsh wind. Awakening from his 'moon dream' (not a daydream), he cheers his spirit up again, telling himself that he is "hardly inferior to many far younger," and treks down the mountain with his step firm and back held high. Such a high spirit of an old man in a song dating back to the 18th century is surely the ideal spirit of "shining old age."

A Scouring Rush Picker

A flake of leaf is whirling down on the wind.
Looking up at the top of the bough.
I notice the traces of the storm there.

Here I am at the Shinano road deep in the mountains
Nosing for special rushes to be used for whetting swords.
The silvery moon of autumn follows me tirelessly
Through the branches of the forest.

My sleeves are wet from the cloak of fog
As I walk through the heavy grasses
Tracking the call of stags.
This is certainly a bracing trek.

I take pleasure in fulfilling my old age in this way
In the hope of deepening
My mind for further enlightenment.
I smile all by myself reading the old anecdote
I share with the pale moon,
The friend of my expedition.

Once upon a time there lived a grandpa and a grandma.
Every morning grandpa went up into the mountains

To collect firewood

And grandma went down to the river

To wash their clothes.

They looked after each other

As they followed their separate ways.

Grandma looked up the mountain

And worried the wind on the ridge

Might be too harsh for grandpa

Without a thought for herself.

They were a long-lived couple.

They turned home everyday together

In a mood of quiet affection.

As a couple we are still getting on well

We are hardly inferior to many far younger.

We can climb even the zigzag road

Or really bad tracks with a rough surface.

Our steps are firm;

Our backs are held high

We trek without a stick,

Exchanging with one another intimate trifling chat.

Autumn Grasses
(Aki no Irokusa)

秋の色種

Lyrics by Toshinari Nanbu
Music by Rokuzaemon Kineya X

Autumn Grasses

This Nagauta was created in 1846 when the Edo culture was in full maturity. Today, Nagauta may be considered by the public to be anything ranging from classical Japanese dance music, to music sung on a stage, to music sung at parties by Geisha girls or by affluent hosts as a part of sophisticated entertainment. If Nagauta had to be categorized under art or hobby, many might categorize it as a hobby. However, I would like everyone to know that there is a Department of Japanese Classic Music in Tokyo University of the Arts teaching Nagauta most extensively. In addition, I hope that the performers will gain their earned artistic status in Nagauta by further enlightening the audience.

The verses in 'Autumn Grasses,' the original expressions of which are quite difficult and complex, were written by a knowledgeable feudal lord named Toshinari Nanbu. According to Dr. Gyokuto Asakawa, the famous researcher of Nagauta, Rokuzaemon Kineya humbled the lord's pride by composing the music to accompany the lyrics with ease. This Nagauta was probably created for the entertainment of the nobles, to be performed in their large mansions which were so clean that not a scrap of dust was to be found. When I was a child, there was a huge house in my neighborhood which belonged to a master of Nagauta, and I remember the songs drifting outside through the thick green trees and bushes covering the garden. 'Autumn Grasses' must have been performed in even more magnificent places.

The whole lyrics are dedicated to the descriptions of beautiful autumnal scenes. Japanese say that a spring evening is worth thousands of times its weight in gold, but if so, an autumn evening must be just as precious. Yet, we would have to say they are both priceless only when used as a background for man and woman to sweetly open their hearts to one another, as is described in the lyrics.

Autumn Grasses

Autumn grasses in the plain
Of the east country cast my thought
On the old life I spent among them.
I live now at the top of the hill of Azabu
Where every evening and every morning
I gaze out on scenes of the moon
And the snow through the door open to the valley.
When a nightingale sings in early spring
I can't help but walk into its melodious world.

Enchanting subtle sounds
Of a woman's kimono, probably
With a pattern of pretty bush clovers
Make you imagine the inside
Of her room behind the screen,
When her clear soaring like a lark's
Trills clearly out of her room.

A high fence of woven brushwood
As tall as the cave is held together
By beautiful autumn grasses.
In the midnight vigil where I share
A pillow with the lovely girl
Leaves sway to the wind

Whisper as though they would tender

Spellbinding words for promise

To the yellow flowers nearby.

Enchanting songs of insects

"Chin chirorin, chin chirorin" weave to my ears

As I rest my head on my arm waiting for the dawn.

There is no happiness the like

Of listening to these insects

Entwining their choral harmonies.

One by one each different tune

Comes in and out without an end

And the grace of their ensemble populates the air.

An ancient Chinese legend tells us

Of a king of the Chu country who, in his dream,

Was in love with a beautiful goddess

Who promised to come back to see him

As a cloud in the dawn,

Or as rain in the night,

With her sleeves soaked in the precious 'Ranja' incense.

Inspired by incense such as that

Man and woman share intimate lusts in words

That are barely heard

And that fade in a dying fall.

Exchange of poetry is an endless joy
For it indulges man and woman.
They sweetly open their hearts
One to another with a lyric sense
Set out on a new journey into love.

Does plucking a *koto* create a sound
Of wind trespassing in the high peaks
Or rough waves overriding rocks?

Let me keep tight in my memory:
The spring of shedding flowers
The autumn of a shining moon
The summer of chirping cuckoos
The winter of falling snow.
As seasons revolve the enchantment goes on forever.

Pine flowers will bloom uniquely
Only once in a hundred years.
Unchanged as the pine trees
Bearing constantly fresh green leaves,
Let us resolve to live long enough
And see the precious flowers of the seasons!
This is the votive offering contained in the song of autumn.

The Wisteria Woman
(Fuji Musume)
藤娘
Lyrics by Genpachi Fujii
Music by Rokusaburo Kineya IV

This Nagauta, said to be composed in 1826, was made purely for the sake of appreciating an accompanying dance performance. The superb performances of "Fuji Musume" by many famous Kabuki masters in the past, such as Kikugoro Onoe Ⅵ, are still being widely talked about, and actors today are still contending with each other in their skill in performing this dance.

Clusters of pretty purple wisteria flowers swinging in the wind resemble beautiful ladies dancing in groups. Together with such imagery of delicate feminine sensitivity, there is also imagery in the lyric which suggests an entirely different aspect of women: boughs of wisteria trees clinging firmly to the trunk of other trees, as though never wanting to let go. The lyric is about those contradictory charms that women possess, which may well contain the answer to why men never cease to be attracted by women. Regardless of age, a man always feels the emotional constraint of his partner, entwining around him like a wisteria bough. A woman can't stop worrying about the wantonness of her man, whose heart she thought she had captured. As the two of them share the same pillow and watch the western sky changing its hue in the dusk, geese fly back to their nests against the background of the setting sun, calling to each other. The last phrases of the lyric remains in our heart like an unforgettable afterglow.

The Wisteria Woman

The memory of spring in Naniwa

Has already sunk far off like a dream of long ago.

Twenty years have elapsed so soon.

I saw many different moons glittering

During those nights never to be forgotten

As they decorated me with tender colours.

Their beauty was beyond description.

I can see my home country now

Covered with autumn foliage.

Let me come home also with fine autumn costume!

Waves of wisteria clusters

Swing in the wind

While their boughs

Cling firmly to the trunk of the pine.

They look like the pine flowers

That may only bloom once in a century.

Avoiding the eyes of others I put on a lacquer hat deeply,

But carry a bough of wisteria on my shoulder

And wear a kimono dyed a wisteria colour

  with a wisteria cluster design

And the ideogram for 'Love' imprinted.

I am so excited that the hem of my kimono
  is easily entangled.

I passed by the Mirror Mountain.

It delivers the message

That one should look at one's own reflection in the mirror

And find out one's own faults

Instead of blaming the faults of others.

I passed by Lake Biwa

When its tide was ebbing even slightly,

Young women divers looked bashful.

What is to be blamed for men

Is that they don't keep their promise

Not to see other women

Though they swear in front of the solemn bells

Of the Mii and Ishiyama Temples.

Are their promises empty cicada shells?

I lie awake many nights in vain.

You get rid of me and wander off to meet other women

As soon as the days warm up and the snow melts

On the road to Mount Hiei.

You provoke my jealousy!

I really don't know how you had the gall to seduce me!

You fail to write though I write to you often.

I almost drown in my many resentments.

Let's plant pine trees in Arima.
They like to be twined by wisteria
In the same way I wish I were
Twined for ever by the languorous of Arima.
My body will be worn out of luscious fatigue
And need more rest.
I will have early evening naps
But they won't suffice.
I would like to sleep longer
Entwined by wisteria.
What shall I do, what shall I do?

How delightful is this wooden pillow!
The pillow of an arm should be
Reliably enchanting too!

The remains of the setting sun
Linger in the hazy sky.
Geese call in flying to their nests
As if they miss the loss of the day.

The New Year Lion Dance—*Section 1 : A Girl Page*
(Kagami Jishi)

鏡獅子（上）小姓の巻

Originates from an old music, "Makura Jishi"
Lyrics by Ouchi Fukuchi
Music by Shojiro Kineya Ⅲ

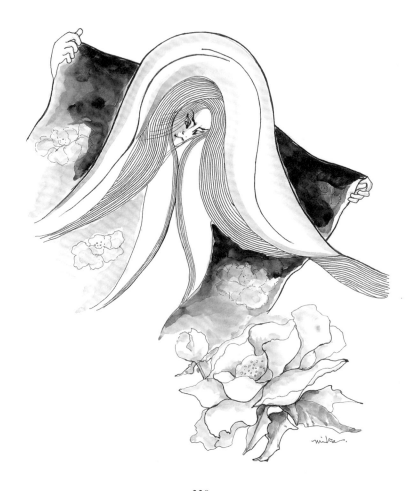

The New Year Lion Dance—*Section 1 : A Girl Page*

Although created in 1893 for a Kabuki dance performance called 'Shun Kyou Kagami Jishi,' it is not appropriate to call this a fairly new Nagauta. The presence of Shishi (lion) in Noh songs goes back a long way; Shishi has been respected as the guardian protecting the mythical stone bridge leading to the holy Mount Tendai in China. In this context, this Nagauta is full of classic and ancient ambience.

A few years after I started Nagauta lessons, my teacher asked me what song I would like to learn next. I replied casually that I might as well try 'Kagami Jishi.' It was just because the performance was on at the Kabuki Theatre then, and I was planning to attend the performance. Hearing this story later, my old mother was taken aback and blamed me for my rudeness, informing me that 'Kagami Jishi' is a song of high status only permitted to be sung by senior singers. When I apologized to my teacher, ashamed of my ignorance, he generously granted me to learn the song. I am still covered in sweat when I recall this incident.

For us Japanese, the image of 'kagami' (mirror) is associated with 'Kagami Mochi,' a round white rice cake in two layers offered to God on the New Year's Day, later eaten by family members on the 11th of January. Probably this is the reason why 'Kagami Jishi' is often performed in the New Year month, or else as a performance given in commemoration of the succession of a stage name.

On the stage, the audience sees a pretty young girl page against a superb background of the inside of Edo Castle. The girl is worried and unhappy to be detached from worldly pleasures and love, which she would be able to enjoy if only

229

not serving the court. Then, to the audience's surprise, the girl becomes possessed by the spirit of the holy lion, the guardian of the sacred stone bridge. The transformed king of animals then starts to dance and chase butterflies, intoxicated by the fragrance of peony flowers. The audience also gets intoxicated by the divine dance of the lion, as the magical combination of song, instruments and stage-set trigger a spiritual experience for the audience, who sees flowers and music falling from the sky as if to signify the appearance of a Buddha.

The New Year Lion Dance—*Section 1: A Girl Page*

You can hear the woodcutters sing in the mountains

And herdsmen blow their horns in the plain,

All of us in this world carry out distinct duties.

I am a girl page serving in the Edo Castle

Detached from the worldly pleasure of love

With all of my adolescent shoots held back

Trotting repeatedly to and fro

Along the huge corridors of the palace

Spending days of endurance on hard duties.

Our legends tell us

The God and the Goddess crossed together

The floating bridge spanning the sky

And opened the way to conjugal harmony.

Since then, the acts of love have spread

With the robust vigour of bamboo roots,

My heart, though, is left in pain

As in the Kawasaki song of the women divers

Working aboard the tiny boats

In the beautiful Ise Bay area;

As drops of morning dew lodge on flower petals

The hearts of all men and women

Are soaked endlessly with the dews of love
Spreading their perfume from fragrant hair,
Little birds say I am a foolish girl
For stubbornly rejecting worldly pleasures
Simply because of my duties in the Palace.
But what else can I choose
Being surrounded all day long
By those heartless court servants?
My pain is as if my comb can't reach
Itchy spots through the heavy hair-do
That comes with the official Palace style.
So all my days have to be steeped in renunciation.

In the spring, people are drawn out
By cherry blossom viewing
And enjoy the lucid sounds of valley streams.
Is it raining? No, it's the wind
Soughing through the pine woods.
I look up at the white clouds and share
The feeling that was told in an ancient story
Of the man who once passed some time
In the sacred Tendai Mountain,
Came back, as he thought, after a stay of only half a day
And found himself among his descendants
Of the seventh generation.

The New Year Lion Dance—*Section 1 : A Girl Page*

Once the season turns, the flowers are gone.

The young leaves come out

  dappling a gentle summer shade.

I love the dance of the Hida Fiesta!

During the rainy May of the lunar calendar

Young girls appear at the paddy

To prepare the soil for planting the rice sprouts,

As they work cheerfully, plenty of water

Is taken into the paddy.

Let's have tea together.

Even those who haven't met before

Can become friends.

Indeed, indeed.

Why don't we stop complaining

Of men who break their promises.

When you give up a man,

You may have an unexpected encounter

With another more to your taste.

Whenever you see and hear him

You will thrill to the touch of love

And the chagrin of my own awkward haste

Not knowing how to cope with him.

Little cuckoos sing in the night of the misty moon.

It is the high season of peonies

Their sumptuous petals are about to fall.

Look, they quietly start to fall, one by one;

Falling one by one in silence.

Falling falling

Falling......

Fascinated

You have no time to sleep.

Why not lie awake all through the night

Watching the grandeur of peonies

And extracting all the trivialities

Of the world out of us!

The full blossoms of peony flowers

Are making waves with the winds

And spreading their fragrance around.

There are scarlet ones, white ones

And pink ones, too.

All together they are the King of the flowers

You never know when it happens

And the little maiden is possessed

By the spirit of the lion! *

(*supplemented by Okumura)

The New Year Lion Dance—*Section 1 : A Girl Page*

The lion is flitting and dancing around the peony,

It now looks the perfect guard

  of the sacred stone bridge.

The bridge looked narrow,

Overhanging and remote well-nigh impossible to cross.

Its surface looks slippery

Because it's covered by heavy moss.

The valley is deep like an entrance to hell.

The stream is cruelly turbulant

With numerous white horses roaring like a storm.

All of a sudden a large melody is heard.

Isn't this a joyful sign of the Buddha's visitation?

Petals are falling from the sky

And flutes and *koto* begin to sound

The clouds glow with the setting sun.

What omens these are of ambient grace!

Acknowledgments

by **Ariyoshi Okumura**

As readers could probably imagine from reading the profiles in the beginning of this book, I am greatly indebted to my two supervisors, my Nagauta teacher, Mr. Takeshi Minagawa of To-on, and the late Mr. François Duchêne, who are the benefactors as well as mentors in my humble aspiration to "artistic elevation" which I have been practicing within the framework of amateurism. They have offered me precious spiritual sustenance that has broadened my mind in the final stage of my life, transcending the genres of Nagauta performance and translation, of which they are specialists. Without their kind advice and consistent support, I would have lost my equilibrium in my reckless attempt to write this book in order to spread Japanese culture abroad, which was certainly far beyond my own bounds. I am also grateful to my ex-teacher, the late Mr. Rikutaro Fukuda, who first taught me English when I was a first year student in the pre-war Tokyo Higher Normal School of Teaching College in 1943. Devoted to the introduction of Japanese Literature abroad as a long-time member of the Japanese National Commission for UNESCO, he was pleased to hear about my translation of Nagauta, and sent me a warm letter to offer his compliments saying my attempt was "an unparalleled unique achievement."

I also want to thank Mr. Yoshiharu Fukuhara (Honorable Chairman of Shiseido Co., Ltd.), the former editor-in-chief of *Hohozue*, a coterie magazine of the Japanese business community of which I am a member, for his heartwarming encouragement, Mr. Toru Haga (Professor Emeritus of the University of Tokyo and former Principal of Kyoto University of Art and Design), Mr. Toru Ajimi (Chairman of Nagauta To-on Kai, Professor Emeritus of Tokyo University of the Arts), and Mr. William P. Malm (Professor Emeritus of Michigan University, USA), who is one of the few foreigners with a deep understanding of Nagauta.

I would like to sincerely thank Ms. Mika Katayama, my friend and artist who studied copper-plate engraving in Paris, has exhibited her works at International Biennial Exhibition of Prints in Tokyo, and whose works are possessed by museums such as MoMA, for creating innovative illustrations for the book.

Last but not least, I am thankful to Ms. Akiko Yamaguchi who helped me translate, among other things, each explanatory note for the lyrics with her English skills as well as her knowledge of Kabuki and Nagauta. She also kindly introduced me Ms. Jenny White formerly of British Council in Japan. She is indeed a superb and dedicating editor with keen interest in Kabuki and Nagauta. I am also indebted to Miyoshi Kikaku who produced this book with his maximum care .

Ariyoshi Okumura
―――*Profile*

Ariyoshi Okumura was born in 1931 in Kobe, Japan. After obtaining a master's degree in applied economics from the University of Tokyo, he started his career at the Industrial Bank of Japan in 1955. He retired from the bank in 1989 as Managing Director and Chief Economist.

During his services as a banker, he spent 1957 and 1958 at the Columbia Business School in New York as a Fulbright Exchange Student, and in 1984, he joined the Advanced Management Program of the Harvard Business School, and had the honor of being the graduation speaker.

In 1960's and 1970's he was actively involved in the governmental effort to ease the US and Japan trade disputes of the time, as an advisor for the ambassadorial envoy, which greatly increased his international acquaintances in later years.

After he finished his Wall Street assignment in 1972, he returned to Japan and started the translation of the lyrics of

Kabuki into English as well as into modern Japanese for the younger generation and for his children, who were raised abroad, and also for a global audience who wish to know more about Japanese traditional culture.

NAGAUTA   *The Lyrics of Kabuki*

2015年8月28日　第1刷発行

翻訳者　　　奥村 有敬 ©2015

　　　　　　山口 晶子

挿　画　　**片山 未加**

製作 発売　美術の図書 三好企画

　　　　　　〒270−0034

　　　　　　千葉県松戸市新松戸1−162　Ａ−102

　　　　　　Tel. 047−347−3211　Fax. 047−347−3222

　　　　　　http://miyoshikikaku.com

印　刷　　祥文社印刷株式会社

落丁本、乱丁本は発行元にてお取替え致します。

著作権法で認められた以外の複写は禁じられています。

Printed in Japan

ISBN 978-4-938740-99-3